DYING TO LIVE

◆ ◆ ◆

The End of Fear

A direct approach to freedom from psychological and emotional suffering

David Parrish

Editor Eliezer Sobel

CONTENTS

Title Page   1

Dedication   5

 FOREWORD   7

INTRODUCTION   11

Approaching this work   15

HOW TO READ THIS BOOK   31

The Condition   33

THE FIRST STEP   40

THE POSSIBILITY   46

THE TEACHING   51

IMAGINE   54

THE FULL CATASTROPHE   61

IGNORANCE   64

FACING IT   76

HAVING ENOUGH   79

BECOMING A SEEKER   83

GIVING UP THE SEARCH   86

NON-DUALITY IS A FACT   89

THE END OF THE SELF AS A PERSON   95

THE FULFILLMENT   101

ON HAVING NO FUTURE   103

NO DEATH   105

THE MIND   109

WHY PRACTICE?   113

THE VALUE OF SUFFERING   118

THE BIG QUESTIONS   122

WHAT IF I DON'T GET IT?   126

WHAT DOES IT ALL AMOUNT TO?   132

THE THREE POSITIONS   136

A NEW PSYCHOLOGY?   139

IS THE RECOGNITION OF the true self enough 141

PRACTICAL STRATEGIES   144

To Jessica with all my love.

FOREWORD

"You are not who you think you are."

From my half century of extensive research as a spiritual seeker, I have concluded that those seven words summarize all of the great mystical traditions and paths to Enlightenment. "The rest is all commentary," said the great Jewish sage, Hillel the Elder.

I am suggesting that all of the spiritual books I have read, and probably you have read, are ultimately about addressing that fundamental statement in some fashion or another. And if it's true that "You are not who you think you are," then the obvious follow-up question is, "Well who am I, then?" Those books and teachings are attempts to answer that question; all of them offer some variation of finding the True Self or God (whichever comes first); or "waking up" to one's True Nature and/or the Ever-Present Divine; or the most popular option, getting Enlightened. All in the hopes of stumbling onto the ultimate release of all suffering and finding ourselves utterly relaxed and nestled inside the Vast Empty Boundless Ground of Being that is both Source of, and One with, All That Is, Was and Will Be.

Or simply "Awareness," as in the case of the present work by Dr.

David Parrish. Or sometimes he calls it "Conscious Awareness." Or the "Self-as-Awareness," "Self-Realization," "Non-Duality," and at one point he even mentions "The Absolute." (Just to keep us on our spiritual toes.) Some teachers simply refer to "It" as "This." Others refer to it as "That." (Take your pick: This or That.)

This principal message, "You are not who you think you are," naturally calls forth its logical concomitant, "Who you *really* are is..." fill in the blank. The answer becomes obvious and clear inside the myriad approaches to discovering the Ineffable, Infinite Consciousness that sits undisturbed, Changeless and Timeless, behind the curtain of this world of 10,000 sorrows.

It also becomes extremely evident that absolutely *nothing* is required to find the object of our seeking, apart from truly grasping those seven simple words and intuiting the radical revolution of the soul to which they point.

Consider:

If "You are not who you think you are"—if that's really and literally true—it changes *everything.*

Thus, I urge you to approach *Dying To Live* with due diligence and a measure of caution, because should you look into your own experience of being human and discover that David's observations contained herein are accurate, then hang on tight as your assumed identity goes on the ride of a lifetime. (Possibly its last ride.)

Dying to yourself in order to "live yourself" fully, to enjoy a "freedom to be" that you only knew as a very young child, will be a completely familiar experience, and not some exotic and magical "state." Which is fortunate, because *all states of mind,* even the mystical, mind-blowing sort, occur in the world of Time, and thus are subject to the laws of the ever-changing flow of events. What we are seeking cannot be a "state," subject to change and dissolution, but rather, must be Eternally rooted in the world of the Changeless, a realm within our own consciousness that *does not come and go*, that is always here, and always now.

Once you know that "You are not who you think you are," and that in fact you are Awareness Itself, you will simultaneously recognize that Awareness has *always* been your True Nature, and it has *never* been missing in action. Therefore, it would seem that no more meditation retreats, exotic practices or books are required to find That which is Always-Already Present.

Well, perhaps just one more.

This one.

Because for most of us, the spiritual path can be a maddening and mind-boggling puzzle: The great teachers insist that there is "nowhere to go and nothing to do"; that who we really are is already whole and complete; and that our True Nature as Awakened Awareness is *always and already the case, here and now*.

And yet, the other half of the puzzle is that most of us nevertheless need to have this essential truth of our Authentic Identity continuously pointed out. Furthermore, we need to *want* this Realization more than anything else in our lives, and re-prioritize accordingly. And yes, we *do* need to do whatever it takes—anything and everything—in order to finally recognize and integrate this most fundamental fact of our existence. Such an insight will at last bring an end to all suffering caused by our mistaken identity and the obscurations of ego that keep it locked in place, and thus allow us to be reborn in a new world of enjoying real freedom to be That whom we have always been.

Dying To Live by my good friend David Parrish is a challenging addition to the body of literature pointing to the True Self. Challenging, in that he asks a lot of the reader; it is hard work. One must persist through frustration, not understanding, and not "getting it." He asks nothing less than that we let go of everything we think we know about ourselves, move through the fear and disorientation such a letting go can provoke, and open ourselves to a new and unexplored possibility for being human.

May it be so, and may all beings be happy, peaceful and free of suffering.

Eliezer Sobel

Red Bank, New Jersey

June 5, 2019

INTRODUCTION

◆ ◆ ◆

E nlightenment is considered a very attractive possibility for many people, especially given the widespread interest in meditation these days, as well as the variety of Eastern teachings and practices that suggest it can be achieved. Beginning in the late sixties, there was a wave of interest in Enlightenment related to the experiences people were having with LSD and the writings of people like Alan Watts, Richard Alpert (Ram Dass), Timothy Leary, and many others. During those times, many spiritual teachers were speaking about Cosmic Consciousness and telling stories of Spiritual Masters who presumably had fully transcended the psychological and emotional suffering common to most human beings. In Ram Dass's spiritual classic, *Be Here Now,* he recounts his tale of finding a Guru in India who appeared to be living inside this extraordinary experience all of the time, and without drugs.

Enlightenment has been defined many different ways, depending on the philosophical background or religious tradition of the person describing it. It can point to the most basic meaning, as simply "lightening up," or it can refer to being a Fully Awakened, Liberated, Realized Being. Generally, though, I think it is fair to say that it commonly refers to having attained essential spiritual knowledge and insight. Many of us who experimented with psychedelics experienced a dimension of consciousness that offered freedom from negative mental states and a clarity that suggested a new way of being that was very fulfilling and in harmony with life. This experience was often exhilarating, profound, and mind-blowing, and at the very least, quite pleasurable and enjoyable. Although for some unlucky souls, their adventure into "better living through chemistry" resulted in nightmarish "bum trips," and often a frightening visit to the psych ward. Needless to say, these were, and are, very powerful substances, not to be trifled with frivolously or without the presence of a qualified guide.

I was a Psychology major in college in the early '70s, and after taking LSD my understanding of reality changed dramatically. The experience of being excited, joyful, and passionate about being alive that I had with LSD was beyond anything I could have ever imagined. I became obsessed with finding anything that could help me understand what had happened. I studied Zen, took the *est* Training, learned Kundalini Yoga, practiced meditation, got into psychotherapy, and hung out with anyone who was interested in being enlightened.

After some time it seemed apparent that I, like most people, was not likely to succeed. Then, when I learned about karma, and that some Eastern traditions believed that it took many lifetimes for people to be enlightened and free of suffering, I concluded that I should just try to make the best of things in this life. I figured that if I could work out my psychological issues, earn a decent living, and be relatively happy, it would be sufficient. Actually, although I *did* succeed in being generally sane and successful in life, as it turned out, it really was *not* sufficient. Over the years I continued to read the ever-growing number of books about spiritual Awakening and Consciousness, practiced meditation and went on retreats.

Then, after many years, I returned from a Buddhist Vipassana meditation retreat and began to experience that I was dying. I was not physically ill; in fact, I was in good health, but I still had a constant awareness or intuition that I was dying. It was a sense that my life was gradually shutting down, and that it would not be long before I was gone. This went on for several months. And then, out of nowhere, I saw that the "me" that was seemingly dying was merely the personality or psychological identity that I had always considered and assumed myself to be. I realized that that identity was not real, and that I had never actually been that identity, and therefore dying was simply recognizing that who I really am was not that "person." And, since that person never actually existed, this death was in fact a rebirth and an awakening to what was actually my true Self.

This was an intense realization: that I was Awareness itself, always present and available but perpetually overlooked because I believed I was this personal character with this specific body, specific past, specific characteristics, and quite mortal. A huge weight was lifted from my psyche and life began to be extremely simple and clear. It seemed to me that I was experiencing the state of Awareness that I had experienced with LSD. I was elated to simply exist and everything seemed obvious.

After this experience, I reread some of the spiritual books I had read in the past, only now my eyes were open in a new way and I was seeing something in them that I had missed. I could not believe that I had somehow overlooked what seemed so obvious to me at that point. It was evident that there was a direct way to Enlightenment. Enlightenment was no longer an abstract, intellectual concept for me, it was now a natural and easeful way of being. It was evident that the key to being Enlightened had to do with seeing the truth of who we are and that this truth is available to anyone at any time.

I had been teaching meditation for many years and now I found myself talking about Self-Realization and the potential we all have to be Enlightened. While I saw meditation as a useful way to slow down, relax the body, and calm the mind, it was now clear to me that true meditation is simply being aware and knowing that you are Awareness itself.

I had written a book called *Enlightenment Made Easy,* based on the work of Douglas Harding, a British philosopher who created a series of experiments that provided direct insight into Conscious Awareness. Harding's experiments revealed a way of "seeing" from Awareness that was very transformative for me. However, it was not until I directly saw the confusion that clouds Awareness that I experienced being Awareness itself and the freedom and fulfillment that it provided. The confusion is a function of our conditioning and the state of mind we live in called being a person, and this is very clearly pointed out by the great teachers and sages, past and present.

This book is a presentation of the basic teaching of Self-Realization. What is pointed to exists as a direct experience that can be confirmed in our everyday lives. I do not expand the teaching with extraneous explanations or examples, but provide core ideas that, if contemplated, can reveal the truth. This endeavor is challenging; it is not just a matter of learning facts or developing understandings. It is a matter of looking inward and seeing the truth behind the conditioned mental state you live in and discovering who you really are. If you accept this possibility and are willing to deal with the complexity of your psychological identity, you can be enlightened. This is really possible and available in this life, and upon realizing it, it will be quite evident that this life is a precious opportunity to awaken to the truth and be happy and free.

APPROACHING
THIS WORK

You have only one life to live and that life is forever.

MOOJI

W e are all dying to live. Everyone wants to be happy and live a fulfilling life. Actually, dying is the most important thing you can do in this life. The death I am referring to is not the death of the body, but a death that will free you to live a life of happiness and fulfillment. It is the death of *who you take yourself to be*: the psychological identity or personality that most people consider to be who they are. Yet who you actually are is *not* a personality, and discovering this can allow you to notice an Awareness that is always present and is the true Self. This Awareness is what looks through your eyes. It is what hears with your ears. It is the pure essence that the Sages and Saints experience, and the realization of this Awareness has been called enlightenment. This realization is possible for all those who recognize this possibility—that they are not who they assume they are—and are willing to let go of their psychological identification that has been formed by conditioning since childhood.

To see the truth of who you are is to bring about an end to the psychological life of the person you are familiar with and refer to as "me," and to realize freedom from the psychological suffering that this confusion brings about. This is a death that paradoxically allows for real life and fulfillment. The truth is that *who you take your self to be is not real*, has no inherent existence, and is only a psychological construct; therefore, *its* death is not *your* death. Its death is an easy death and a good death because it *reveals the truth of who you are*: the Self, or timeless and ever-present Awareness that is your true nature. This Self is inherently aware, real, awake, and free from suffering. So the dying being referred to is actually a rebirth. The intention to let go of the identity that you have taken yourself to be, and to see that it has never been who you really are, opens the door to freedom and happiness. And, since this identity was never actually in existence other than as a thought or concept, its death is nothing other than a recognition of the truth.

If you see this possibility, or even if you're just curious to find out what it is all about, then give consideration to the often challenging material presented in this book.

Do you know who you are? Don't answer too quickly. I am not talking about the common ways that people identify themselves: I am a man or a woman; I am a father or mother; I am a human being, etc. If you stand in front of a mirror and look into the eyes you see there, who is it that is looking through those eyes? Suppose that what is looking through those eyes is the key to happiness and well-being? And what if who you have assumed yourself to be is the very obstacle to that happiness and well-being? Not that who you think you are is "wrong," or a problem; it is just not actually who you are. Instead, it is who you learned you are during infancy and childhood, or who you took yourself to be given the roles you play or your physical appearance.

I am asserting that who you really are is happy, content, peaceful, fully alive, and at ease in life.

I expect that for most of us that does not seem at all true. Just stay with me and give this assertion a chance. And I am also asserting that what's preventing you from having this joyful experience of yourself is simply a mistaken idea you learned and believed about who you are. That is all that needs to be seen to begin to awaken to your true identity and the expansive life that it offers. Don't worry, you have plenty of company. Most of humanity is suffering from this confusion along with the trouble it causes.

In my career as a psychologist, I have worked with thousands of people suffering from various forms of distress and dysfunction, and I have dedicated my life to serving them through whatever means I could find that would alleviate their suffering and promote well-being. After decades of frustration, because conventional psychotherapy was so limited, I finally discovered the key to well-being. This key focuses on the root cause of suffering rather than the many ways that suffering manifests. This root cause has to do with *identity*, or who we actually are in essence. And when this is seen it becomes clear that to let go of who we think we are is the way to freedom and the fulfillment of our potential.

What is contained here has the potential to bring an end to all psychological and emotional suffering. This is an incredible claim, yet if the possibility illuminated here is followed and given consistent attention and contemplation, it will prove to be true. Much of what will be presented points to a simple truth. However, seeing this truth involves dealing with ideas that may appear difficult to grasp. This is due to the existing way of thinking and understanding that is an aspect of our universal human condition. There is a tendency to resist information that contradicts the way we have understood who we are and what is real. Therefore, to gain the power and value of what is presented here, you will need to stay open and give due consideration to the material with patience and focus. It may take getting far enough into this book to begin to see what I am pointing at. Do yourself a favor and stay with it, even when you might feel frustrated and want to put the book down, or even fling it across the room. In the end you will find that is was well worth your time and energy.

What will be presented here is consistent with the highest teachings of the Saints, Master, Sages, and Gurus throughout the ages, and it can transform and transcend the everyday dysfunctional life that most of humanity is mired in.

The key points in this teaching will be repeated in various ways because the truth is not linear, it is holistic, so don't be concerned if you see repetition, but rather, allow what is presented to continue to marinate as you consider, reflect, and contemplate it. Try not to turn this over to the mind; that is, don't just think about it and try to arrive at some conclusion. See if you can just allow the message to reveal itself as you go.

Human suffering has been the subject of philosophical and religious dialogue for many centuries. What is meant by suffering here is not the common everyday challenges and situations that arise in life, or the physical pain that we all encounter at various times, but rather, the chronic conditions of anxiety, depression, and frustration, or loneliness and despair, along with all of the destructive behaviors that result from these conditions. This suffering is not evident to some people because their comfortable circumstances often mask the instability and vulnerability that lie beneath the surface. Or they are so deluded into believing that they are in control and happy with material and temporary gratifications that they are able to ignore the underlying reality. No matter how comfortable or deluded a person may be, life will eventually present the unavoidable truth. No one escapes the unpredictability of life, or the inevitable effects of time and change. We will all experience sickness, loss, emotional instability, old age (if we make it that far), and death.

Many of the Gurus and Masters of Eastern teachings and practices seemed to have gotten to a consistent state of well-being and fulfillment, but how this came to be was not at all clear. It is often said that meditation is a way to increase the probability of experiencing such a state, but among the multitude of people who have practiced meditation, it has not seemed to work with any degree of consistency. So while meditation can sometimes produce a calmer mind and increased awareness, there is something other than meditation that is the key to discovering Awareness to be our true nature.

Over time, a few beings have spoken of a possibility for liberation or freedom from suffering. Much of what was shared by these beings has been misunderstood and distorted to fit the prevailing state of mind. There was a tendency to create fixed teachings and practices by followers of such teachers. Often what the originator intended was lost and converted to an ideology that must never be questioned, at all costs, even to the point of death to "heretics."

In recent times there have been a few of these "liberated beings" who have shared a specific possibility that is consistent with the original intentions of the greatest Masters and Sages. The essence of what they have shared is that most of humanity has followed a mistaken idea of who and what they are, leaving people in a limited mental, emotional, and physical state that is subject to suffering and is at odds with life. It is so thoroughly embedded in the human brain and mind that it is a blind spot for most human beings. Those who recognize this mistake yearn for freedom and seek to realize an enlightened state of being: to simply discover what is always present to be realized, and which is commonly ignored. This discovery is a direct, first-person experience that opens up a new way of being that is naturally happy and fulfilled. This is not a magical or even religious claim, it is simply the truth. It is the discovery of Conscious Awareness, always present in the background as the actuality of who we are.

When I look at humanity, what I see is that every human being is consistently seeking the same experience. We all strive for well-being in the form of freedom from fear, fulfillment in relationships, a sense of security and peace, and some way of being that is not at odds with the realities of life; in other words, an experience of acceptance and fulfillment. Even the most horrendous forms of human behavior seem to be based on an underlying—usually unconscious—attempt to realize some form of existence that provides relief from the struggles and challenges of life.

I encourage you to open yourself to the ideas offered here, ideas that will provide you with the genuine possibility of being happy and at home in this life. This is beyond therapy; it is a process of "seeing"—by which I mean "internally observing"—that provides a natural evolution beyond conditioning and limited ways of being. It is not beyond the reach of anyone willing to engage with these teachings and practices. In my work as a psychologist who has assisted thousands of people over five decades, I struggled to produce results with patients using conventional, therapeutic approaches. But it wasn't until I began approaching my work with clients from this unconventional, yet effective approach that I finally started seeing significant, lasting results.

This book is written to provide relief to people who are suffering from the various psychological and emotional problems that arise from the limited and false ways that we have been educated about who we really are. That includes almost all of us. The collective experience we share is one where we find ourselves having difficulty with our states of mind, emotions and unworkable behaviors. This is accepted as "just the way people are," or "the way life is," because most of us are completely unaware of what is possible. I am proposing that the source of the mental and emotional conditions that interfere with a fulfilling life is the confused and limited awareness of who and what we truly are. This is not a matter of philosophy or spiritual development. It is a matter of simply seeing beyond the limited view that we have as a conditioned personality and recognizing the true and natural Self.

It is of great importance that people realize that it is not inevitable that life is experienced with apprehension and constant discontent and disturbance. Whether you are someone who considers yourself to be generally managing life successfully and dealing well with stress, or you are someone who is suffering from anxiety, depression, or some degree of dysfunction in your relationships or work life, there is a way to see yourself and your life that can make a profound difference in the quality of your daily experience. It is not a matter of how academically advanced you are, nor whether you fully understand all of what is presented here about the possibility of well-being. What will make the difference is your willingness to maintain an open mind and having a genuine commitment to your well-being. If that is indeed the case, then the consistent exposure to the possibility presented here—the reality of being fully awake and aware—will reveal itself to you. It is only the limited state of mind and the constraints of having been conditioned by a culture and educational system poorly designed for well-being that block a clear, aware view of who we are. Most conventional psychology is a product of this limited view of our identity, and this is why it cannot produce a way to be free of the mental conditions that so many of us endure. As has been noted by leading thinkers and philosophers, the problems that arise from a limited system cannot be resolved inside that same system.

I have always considered my own life to be the most useful laboratory for testing approaches to psychotherapy. Many people consider the practice of meditation to be a path to awakening and freedom. Although meditation was clearly valuable to me in learning to regulate my mental states, it did not actually make a significant difference in the way I experienced myself and my life. Patterns of thoughts and emotions continued to result in irrational behavior and difficulty in relationships, and my overall experience of life continued to be one of apprehension and uncertainty. I had not come to a consistent experience of well-being or happiness. I also engaged, as a client, in many forms of therapy with excellent therapists, to learn about the current models being used, as well as to work on my own psychological life. The advantage was that I recognized myself to be essentially "normal." That is, I functioned as well as most people while sharing the same neurotic tendencies. Over the years I had contact with many psychologists and psychiatrists, and I was often shocked by how many of them were minimally functional in their own lives. I came across people providing treatment who were worse off than many of their clients. It seems that most people in the human behavior business accept the assumption that neurosis and various degrees of dysfunction and instability are "normal."

Perhaps it was because I had had the mind-expanding experiences provided by psychedelic drugs, and I had explored Eastern ideas early in my life, that I sensed there was something unseen that could be the key to experiencing life as fulfilling. Or perhaps the experience of freedom and enjoyment that I had during and after a powerful course I attended in the '70s called the "*est* Training" contributed to what seemed possible. But, as is the case with all peak experiences, these pleasurable and expanded states did not last. Still, it seemed to me that if such experiences could happen even once, it might be possible for them to be more consistent. I just did not see how. There have been periods in my life when I had spontaneous moments of enjoying a natural sense of clarity and well-being. There didn't seem to be a specific thing that I did to bring those on, and they usually lasted from a few days to a few weeks, but always gradually morphed back into the typical neurotic life. This also seemed to be the case for others who have had temporary periods of expanded states of consciousness.

It seemed that the typical personality structure of the clients I saw in my practice was generally rigid and embedded in habit patterns that were not only resistant to change, but seemed to actively counteract any and all attempts to disrupt them. The only thing that did seem to work was not the application of "best practice" therapy models, but rather, simply educating clients about the way the mind works, and assisting them in maintaining focused awareness. It became evident to me that awareness itself was the most crucial factor in the therapeutic process. In the light of Conscious Awareness, confusion, reactive mental patterns, and misunderstandings seemed to fall away naturally.

However, I was not yet clear about "awareness." I pondered what this awareness really is. How does it relate to the personality and the patterns of thoughts, feelings, and behaviors that appear to dominate people and result in unworkable, adverse outcomes and debilitating psychological conditions? And how might I work with people to assist them in remaining more consistently aware in a way that would empower them?

I could see that meditation is one practice that is clearly related to being aware. I practiced and taught meditation, and I brought it into play whenever it seemed appropriate in my psychotherapeutic work. However, in many cases, given the personality type and the psychological condition of the client, it was not a realistic option. Even when it was clearly appropriate to the person, most clients were not able to establish a consistent meditation practice. And, as stated prior, even when practiced regularly, it did not produce a lasting state of well-being and fulfillment.

◆ ◆ ◆

The Discovery

23

I eventually discovered a profound possibility available to all human beings, a discovery consistent with thousands of years of teachings and practices, yet of interest to only a fraction of humanity. I predict that over time these teachings will become the basis of a new form of resolving psychological and emotional suffering.

All of the psychological and therapeutic solutions that have come along have not really made a significant difference in the lives of most people. So that brings a question: Is it really possible to experience life in a happy, calm, and peaceful state? Or is it simply that life is a futile dilemma that is so unpredictable and unstable that it is unrealistic to expect to have any lasting happiness and peace?

I discovered that freedom from the suffering that is common to most people is actually much easier to achieve than is usually suspected. This appears to be almost totally unrecognized by most human beings—*and therapists!*—a fact that is hard to believe, given all of the energy that has gone into relieving human suffering. I am asserting that ending human suffering involves a straightforward truth that is hidden from view by our preoccupation with what most of us consider to be true. It is said that the truth will set you free; I suggest that you will find this truth to be a very surprising discovery.

After many years of study and practice, the secret of Awareness finally became clear to me. What I saw was a shock, in that I could not believe I had missed it for so long. It seemed so obvious once it was seen, and it was the final answer! I had found that to practice being aware, mindful, and attentive to what was happening, moment to moment, provided clarity and access to the ability to intervene in negative states of mind and dysfunctional patterns of behavior. What I had missed for so long was that it is not just a matter of being aware, but one of recognizing that I *am* Awareness, and that the mistaken idea that I was a personality was the source of all of my psychological and emotional suffering. Once I saw this, it was clear that this had always been the truth and that the illusion of considering myself to be a separate "person"—identified with a body, a story, and a state of mind—was an illusion. This Self-Realization opens the door to a consistent and reliable way of being in the world. Awareness does not come and go, and it is not defined by a particular experience. To be the Awareness that we actually are is to wake up and "see" life as it is.

This idea that you are Awareness may seem abstract or may not make sense to you. This is because we are so profoundly identified with being a person and a body, and Awareness is not physical, not a thing, so how can we be that? In fact, although it is evident that Awareness exists, we see Awareness as an attribute or quality of who we are, i.e., "I am aware." So the idea that Awareness is who we are requires a willingness to slow down and "look" so that we can "see" what is actually so. When we state that "I am aware," we are actually saying that the idea of who I am is aware. This is a mistake. The person or idea of who we are exists *in* Awareness. What we call the person, image, or concept of who we are is unstable, unreliable, and constantly changing. Our thoughts and feelings are constantly changing, whereas Awareness always remains stable and reliable; it never changes, it exists at all times, and it has been our Ground of Being all along. Awareness was there before we learned our names and before the body was considered to be what we were. As you consider what follows, it will begin to become evident that what you are discovering has been overlooked by most of us.

If we are Awareness, then it would make sense to ask, "Why don't we know that?" We don't know that because when we enter the world, we take on a physical identity. Birth is the embodiment of Awareness in a world of time, space, and form.

We learn to take on the identity of being a person, playing roles, and taking our place in the world. As time passes, this all seems obvious and accurate as our reality, and we slowly learn that we are mortal and that life begins and ends and that we have to make the best of it. Human suffering seems to be inevitable given the facts of life. We are subject to a world we cannot control. We face danger and threats, grow old, experience sickness and pain. And in the end, we all meet our demise. Many find solace in religious beliefs that offer faith in an afterlife. Others live for today, seeking pleasure, material security, a position of power, recognition and control. Distractions such as entertainment of all sorts, food and drink, and sex become highly valued and promoted as aspects of a good life. Physical and mental disease and dysfunction are prevalent in such a world, and fear in the form of anxiety and destructive, reactive behaviors dominate humanity in the form of war, crime, and corruption.

If you are willing to consider the possibility of freedom from suffering and all of what opens up for an awakened being, this book will be of use.

I have discovered that not only is it possible to be free from universal psychological suffering and the seeming futility of life, but the realization of this freedom is among the easiest and direct of all possible paths.

Paradoxically, this is what makes it so elusive.

It seems so elusive because Awareness as the truth of who we are is *already the case.* Therefore, we do not have to *become* Awareness. We don't even have to change anything, other than to begin to pay attention and recognize, from moment to moment, that we *are* Awareness.

What can complicate this is that the mind will present thoughts, feelings, and physical sensations that attract our attention and draw us back into the mistaken identity of being a person. When this happens, we fall out of knowing ourselves as Awareness, and back into the view of ourselves from the perspective of a person. Then what is happening is no longer merely a neutral event happening in Awareness, to be noticed and allowed, it is happening to "me," and thus takes on a personal and much more weighty significance. It has become a problem we need to solve or get rid of. This is a habit pattern and is bound to occur for a while until we are established as Awareness. It will be seen that since we have never actually been the "person" other than taking on that identity as a part of coming into the existing world, we need not *do* anything to end the confusion other than to be aware of Awareness as the truth of who we are. Said another way, *you need not get out of a situation you were never actually in.*

What further complicates this is that while you are not what you think you are, you do not know how to be what you are. The experience of who you are is hidden by the notion that you are some "thing," such as a body. We use our thoughts, feelings, and actions to infer that we are the thing that thinks, feels, and acts.

Even though there is no actual evidenvce that this is the case.

Thoughts, feelings, and actions *happen*—they occur spontaneously, of their own accord—and the mind claims them as not only coming from us, but under our jurisdiction to do something about them. But it is possible to see that this is not the case, that we are not actually the source of thoughts, or feelings; that they have a life of their own.

I am offering an invitation to freedom. The ideas I present here are not new. This time-honored perspective and approach has escaped recognition by nearly everyone, everywhere, because the state of mind in which most of humanity experiences life remains fixed and seems to be all that there is. Many believe these ideas to be impractical, esoteric, or mystical. In many cases, these teachings and practices have been embedded in religious beliefs or abstract philosophical ideology; this has made them seem more a matter of speculation or merely faith-based views. In fact, what these teachings point to is simply the objective truth, and this truth is evident to each of us when we give it our attention with an open mind. Not because I or anyone else said so, but because it can become evident to *you* in your own direct experience.

In order to present these teachings and instructions in a way that is free from the spiritual trappings that have resulted in confusion and unnecessary sidetracks, I will avoid the use of spiritual language or references to specific teachings, religious or otherwise, although what is presented here is totally consistent with the essence of all spiritual traditions.

To be clear, I am asserting that all human beings can be free from suffering, and this freedom is readily available at all times. Whether it is a matter of wanting to be free from anxiety, depression, addiction, or from failed relationships, there is a direct way that works to end all forms of suffering. This path is free and does not require any previous preparation, joining any group or organization, or departure from ordinary life.

If you give full attention and maintain an open mind as you read and contemplate the material presented here, you will have all you need to realize freedom. Upon seeing what is possible you will be moved by an intelligence that will guide you to fulfill the potential you have to be fully awake, alive, free, peaceful, and happy.

As I stated earlier, I tend to repeat certain concepts and ideas throughout the book. This is intentional. The message being transmitted here is being spoken directly to Awareness, which is your true Self. It is this Awareness that will respond and reveal itself. The repetition is intended to get past the mental state that receives new incoming information and considers whether it is relevant to the "person." This is the most challenging aspect of this teaching. The mental state which is the identity we call "I" or "me" is processing what is presented as information about the possibility of "it" getting free. The identity (who we consider ourselves to be) will hear what is said to imply that it is possible to be free *in the future,* if certain conditions are met or if certain actions are taken. This will, in a sense, neuter the message, because it will claim it to be about itself and thus derail the possibility of the message revealing the true Self, which can never show up in the future, because it is always already present.

Most questions that come up about this way of realization come out of this confusion. The listener, or reader, is attempting to understand and find out what to do from the point of view of the person (without noticing it). As long as this is the case, the person is in a state of delusion in which the person is trying to be free, trying to *become* Awareness, which is already present and observing this entire dilemma. As was stated by a well-known teacher: "There is a presupposed non-existing self that is trying to get salvation for the non-existing self." At some point, if this is recognized and the attention is redirected to Awareness, it is seen that this is a ruse and the veil of ignorance will drop.

My favorite piece of writing on the topic of Self-Realization is in a book by Alan Watts called *The Supreme Identity.* In this book, Watts talks about the "Way of Realization." He points out that: "To become, or realize, what we are, we must first try to become it, in order to realize effectively that is not necessary to do so." He also states: "Realization comes only when the Self wills it freely, without necessity." You see, the Self does not *need* to realize itself, it is always already aware of itself. So when the attempts by the person to try to realize the Self fail, and it is subsequently seen that nothing need be done because the realization of Self-as-Awareness is already the case, then Realization is confirmed. Watts goes on to say: "Realization of the Supreme Identity is found, not through seeking it as remote and obscure, but in ac-

cepting the truth that nothing is more obvious and self-evident."
It is imperative to see that the person cannot realize the Self, but
the Self can be aware of the person, as a finite manifestation of
itself. This immediately reveals the obscuration and the lights go
on (enlightenment).

If you accept this message and the invitation and come to see the
truth, you will recognize that both the invitation and the message are an expression of our shared True Nature. This discovery
will enable you to live from the truth and will open up a future
that could not have occurred without escaping the veil of ignorance and recognizing the reality of who you really are as Awareness itself. This message and the available realization is nothing
short of a miracle. The miracle of Self-Realization.

HOW TO READ
THIS BOOK

◆ ◆ ◆

T he common way of understanding can be an obstacle to the realization that Awareness is the true Self. What is re- quired to connect with the truth of who we are is direct recognition.

What is being pointed to cannot be spoken of or seen as an object of perception, it can only happen as a discovery. Thus, much of what is said here may not make sense, because we ordinarily con- sider what exists and what is real to be material,i.e., a thing or object to be seen. In the case of Awareness there is no object and yet it is possible to notice it. The directing of attention back to its Source is intended to stimulate a direct recognition of what is and has always been what you are. Therefore, there is nothing to learn, no result to be had, nothing to get, and no specific path to get there. To wake up is to see that who you actually are has never been asleep. To see that the you that you think you are doesn't actually exist is to see who you really are, because your false iden- tity of personhood is seen *from* there.

The way to read this book that will stimulate the potential to see this is just to read the words and contemplate what they suggest without making an effort to understand, learn, or come to know anything. Take what is said and look to see Awareness. If you take what is said this way it will begin to reveal itself, through a sense of awe and gratitude that arises, and life will begin to appear easy. It will begin to be clear that to be yourself and to be here, is to be no-thing and to be no-where. Awareness is not a thing, thus no-thing (nothing), and Awareness is like space so it has no position, thus it is no-where (nowhere).

Awareness is non-conceptual and non-phenomenal. To speak about it is only of use as a pointer since it cannot be seen, only known by itself as itself. That which is looking can never be seen as an object of perception, because it is the very place where the looking is coming from. It is the same reason that an eye cannot see itself.

What this book is about has already happened, so the only barrier to being what you are is to notice it. Words are like a song or a poem that suggest Awareness. The words can evoke a feeling or sense of it, just as a song or poem can stimulate an experience.

Intention fuels the awakening. Perhaps more than anything, the desire and intention to be awake and to be free manifests in a paradox: the person wanting to be free from itself. This is dying to live. The willingness, intention, and desire to end the identification as a person begins the process of awakening that results in the birth of a *conscious human being, i.e., a human being that embodies and expresses Awareness.*

This is an invitation to see what is already so. Nothing else really matters. It has been said that this is the purpose of a human life: to awaken to the freedom of being, and to feel the incredible lightness of being.

THE CONDITION

DYING TO LIVE: THE CONDITION

◆ ◆ ◆

W e all share a brief period of time on this earth. For thousands of years the majority of human beings have come and gone and played a part in the drama of their time. As Shakespeare said:

Tomorrow, and tomorrow, and tomorrow,
Creeps in this petty pace from day to day,
To the last syllable of recorded time
And all our yesterdays have lighted fools
The way to dusty death. Out, out, brief candle!
Life's but a walking shadow, a poor player,
That struts and frets his hour upon the stage,
And then is heard no more. It is a tale
Told by an idiot, full of sound and fury,
Signifying nothing.

Is the life most of humanity lives the only reality? Is it possible to discover a truth beyond the agreed upon reality that offers an experience of freedom from the seeming inevitable suffering in a human existence? Is it foolish to search for fulfillment?

◆ ◆ ◆

What is it that explains the way life is for most of humanity? It seems as though suffering, injustice, conflict, and many forms of violence is the very nature of human beings. There are the overt and obvious forms of conflict and violence in the world, and there are subtle forms of conflict within our own minds that result in our doing violence to ourselves, in the form of neglecting our well-being, acting out anger, or withdrawing into isolation. Is it possible there's an explanation for all of this suffering that perhaps has not gotten attention or acceptance?

The field of psychology has established that who we are is the result of DNA, our past experiences, and the formation of a personality that is either healthy and functional or disordered and dysfunctional. This field was developed primarily by studying behavior, applying a system of cause and effect that uses repeatable experiments to verify theories. Most people consider themselves to *be* a personality and behave consistent with that belief, which is based on conditioning and the accepted idea that human beings are psychological entities. This fits the realm of scientific knowledge in that what can be observed and measured proves that the theories and conclusions are accurate descriptions of what is real. Human behavior can be observed and measured and this behavior can be understood as the "psychological makeup" of the person. If we are left with this as our understanding of who we are, it puts us in a very limited condition that results in a plethora of psychological and emotional suffering.

This personality (psychological construct) is constantly changing in reaction to the environment, based on past experiences. In addition, the patterns of behavior that are formed and stored in the brain replay in a mechanical and automatic way that makes behavioral change very challenging. Given this dynamic, and the fact that people tend to justify and defend their behaviors, most psychologists agree that it is unrealistic to expect dramatic changes to occur in psychotherapy, especially if the person is suffering from extreme disorders. And yet there have always been cases of people who appear to experience a radical transformation that changes not just problematic behaviors but the very essence of who they are.

For thousands of years there have been those who have come upon the possibility of freedom from the suffering that pervades the common story of a human life. People have come together in every period of time to engage with the possibility of such a discovery, one that offers peace, fulfillment, and freedom from psychological suffering. It comes to some in desperate times; for others it appears in the course of everyday life circumstances; and for some, it comes in the form of meeting someone who has realized this possibility of freedom.

There is no clear pattern to how people come into contact with this possibility. Many consider it a matter of "grace," which is a very abstract idea. Grace has to do with receiving a blessing that is not a result of any actions taken, nor earning and deserving it, but just as a gift that is bestowed without reason. One way of understanding grace is that it comes into play when the "person" lets go of the belief that they know who or what they are, and opens to the possibility of discovering that who they are can be revealed by simply looking at who or what it is that they have been referring to as "I."

It is possible to be free from psychological and emotional suffering and to experience life in a completely new way.

This freedom has been realized by only a few people over many thousands of years, and the teachings and practices associated with this discovery and realization have been considered a matter of religious or esoteric teachings that were not readily available to most people. These teachings and practices were considered mysterious and not relevant to the general population, or related to the reality that was considered to be the absolute truth. Ironically though, the primary religions of the world were actually based on the teachings of such Realized beings who, along with their message, were considered to be supernatural. And, the experience and vision that these Realized beings expressed was considered a rare phenomenon.

Today, however, the most direct teaching for "waking up" to the truth of who and what we are is available to anyone who is interested. There are teachers who have made it available to the masses via the Internet. As these teachings were passed on by contemporary masters, they have been translated into language and concepts that are comprehensible to most people today. It is now possible for any human being to learn about the possibility of freedom from the pervasive human state of mind and discover a state of being that is inherently fulfilling and free from suffering; it is possible for any human being to transcend the world generated by ignorance and live in freedom, peace, and well-being.

Once there is an awareness of the limitations of living as a psychological identity that continues to perpetuate patterns based on past traumas and rigid conditioning, it becomes evident that such a life is unacceptable. When there is a willingness to look beyond the common view of what it is to be a human being, there is a possibility of escaping the sense of futility that comes as time passes and all of the ways to achieve lasting happiness and peace have failed. How long must a person continue to grasp at what appears to provide fulfillment and never does, before it becomes evident that something is missing? When there is a readiness and an open mind, the possibility presented here is a discovery that reveals the actual cause of suffering and the way to freedom.

This discovery is at the heart of what it is in truth to be human. It begins with the recognition that it is a fundamental failure not to realize that we are not in actuality what we have been conditioned to believe we are. While it may be necessary to take on an identity to participate in the world of individual people who interact with names and roles, this identity is not who we actually are. The process of taking on being a person is a process of learning to be identified with a body, a personality, roles to play, a place in the social world, etc. This learning to be a person is the process of being brought into the existing tribe of humanity based on the particular family, country, language, customs, beliefs, and culture into which one is born. Prior to language, which is the means of learning to be a person, the infant is simply existing as an aware and conscious being that is immediately related to what is happening in every moment. After learning to be a person, the being lives in an *interpretation* of what is happening, produced by thought, which is the mental language that processes what is happening through the filter of conditioning and experience. This becomes who the being considers itself to be: a person in the world of persons.

It is critical to "see" that this person is a psychological construct, and not actually the truth; that is, it does not have an inherent existence, but exists only as a thought, belief, or idea within Awareness. And while this "person" is a manifestation of Awareness, it is a very limited, unstable, ever-changing facade that finds itself challenged by a world too complex to comprehend, a world that presents constant threats to the stability and safety of the person. This results in an ongoing effort to establish security through material wealth, psychological strategies such as manipulation, denial, and domination through a variety of means, including physical domination, control of resources, and emotional pressure. This constant effort is never-ending because all of humanity is competing and all of humanity is operating from a fear-based, psychological state of mind, which processes all that happens in order to determine whether there is a threat, or the prospect of pain or pleasure.

Such a limited, unstable, and stressful life requires constant attention, and results in mental and physical disorders and desperate attempts to escape. This is why distractions have become so important to most of humanity, such as TV, movies, the Internet, social media, and spectator sports. While these activities can have an appropriate place in life, most people in developed countries work hard merely to pay for the time to distract themselves. And then there are the ways to alter mood and attempt to control states of mind with alcohol, legal and illegal drugs, overeating, and preoccupation with sex. These activities are promoted by media and commercial agents as desirable ways to experience life. It is seldom recognized that they provide distractions from the dissatisfaction and anxiety that is underneath the daily pretense of well-being.

If the teachings and practices that offer freedom are pursued, and the possibility of freedom is seen as the only way to experience the natural state of well-being and happiness, then the possibility begins to become a probability. What is unreal will give way to the truth and the limited, unstable pretense that is commonly considered the self will begin to dissolve. This is the death of an illusion and the end of ignorance. Once this possibility is seen, it becomes clear that "dying to live" is to be free of the constriction of being a person and to realize the endless expanse and joy of being alive.

In the context of the teachings for Self-Realization, death is the end of the illusion of being a person. This death is not real because the person never truly existed in the first place. Death then, is the end of ignorance, because in order to maintain the existence of a person it is necessary to ignore the reality of who we really are. When this death occurs, nothing "happens" because it is merely the death of what did not exist.

To understand this is to want nothing more than to die, and this death is the end of suffering; this dying is dying to live. It is the beginning of the fulfillment of a human life.

This book is an invitation to freedom. What is shared is an expression of the various aspects of Self-Realization. The intention is to provide material to contemplate and to look and recognize what is true. When one is established in this "seeing," the truth is obvious.

Do not be deterred by confusion or mental reactions. Read what is offered here with an open mind and an open heart and it will reveal itself to you. Being what you are is simple and easy; letting go of what you're not can involve complications. This is why guidance is so valuable.

If the possibility offered here is clearly seen, and there is sufficient maturity to recognize that nothing short of realizing this possibility will provide the fulfillment of all that humanity desires, there will be a natural impulse to move toward the truth. This impulse will be the movement of life energy into the heart, the heart that is the ever-present reality of the Absolute.

Give time and patience to reading this book and use it as a gateway to what is a natural state of being that is final, timeless, unchanging, unborn, and is the source of everlasting peace and joy.

THE FIRST STEP

◆ ◆ ◆

The "person" is a concept or image that we have of ourselves. It is who or what we consider ourselves to be. We identify with the body as "my body," and we live with the assumption that we remain the same person over time. This is simply not the case. Our bodies are always changing and as we age we change in many dramatic ways, so this person that we think we are is not at all consistent. Likewise, thoughts, feelings, and sensations are also changing all of the time. There is no stability or consistency in the life of a person.

This is why the experience of being a person is complicated and often uncomfortable. What we believe changes, how we see ourselves changes, how we see others changes. What you love can become what you hate. What you believed could be seen as nonsense at another time. This inconsistency is the source of insecurity and even depression when it is seen that nothing can be counted on to stay the same. We change, the people around us change, and the world changes. It seems that nothing is permanent in this life. That is, until we discover the True Self, which doesn't come and go, and is the only constant we can rely on.

Until and unless it is clearly seen that who you consider your self to be *actually* does not exist other than as a concept maintained in thought, there will be no foundation from which to awaken to the truth of who you are. This is not to say that the person you appear to be in the world does not exist. The "person" is a *learned identity* that has developed over time. The problem is that people consider it to be actually real and who they are, and more importantly, they do not realize that this mistaken identity is the source of all their psychological and emotional suffering.

This recognition is the first and most important step in bringing about the end of the illusion that has dominated humanity.

This step is not possible as an intellectual realization. In fact, it can only occur as a movement of the only actual and real Self. This awakening is often attributed to what is called "Grace." The definition of Grace that I am using here is: *the free and unmerited favor of God, as manifested in the bestowal of blessings.* While this concept is typically associated with Christian teachings, it is a useful term in understanding how Self-Realization occurs.

The idea that God is the source of the Realization of Self brings into play the notion that our true Self *is* God. Many people cannot accept this notion. For most people, God is separate from who they are and it is even considered blasphemous to consider oneself to be God. This is due to the identification with the self as a separate and limited entity that is not aware of its Source. It is also the view of many religions, and severely limits the power and value of such belief systems. Although, in the hidden, mystical teachings of all the great religious traditions, the idea that we are God is totally accepted and considered to be the truth. Mystical, meaning: spiritually allegorical or symbolic; *transcending human understanding.* This transcending of human understanding refers to a view of the human experience that sees that Conscious Awareness, within which the limited identity or person exists, is the Source of Reality itself, and as such is obviously a fitting description of God.

If one can move beyond the difficulty with understanding God, the appreciation of what Grace is can be useful in understanding the nature of Self-Realization. As long as the separate, limited, and mistaken identity you think you are is the one who is attempting to realize the Self, so as to be free of the limitations and difficulties of life, Realization is not possible. When the truth of who you really are as Awareness Itself is seen as real and undeniable, *without* attempting to escape the limitations of the false person, then Self-Realization can occur. This could be called "surrender," or letting go of the notion that one knows who they are, as well as letting go of all that such an identity brings with it. And letting go of the deeply-held assumption that *something must change* before we can possibly be happy and free. This letting go is by the "Grace of God."

This would be a letting go of "my" will and substituting the will of God, as in, "Thy will be done." This explains the dilemma of the "seeker." As long as the seeker chases after truth in order for who they are as a person to experience freedom or salvation, they are inadvertently undermining the possibility of Realization. When those who claim to have come to freedom share what happened, it typically—and paradoxically—involves a period of experience when they totally gave up the idea that they would *ever* attain freedom. It is also important to let go of the notion that one has to earn or be worthy of freedom or the Realization of the True Self or God. To realize what you already are and have always been cannot be dependent on any condition. *Nothing has to change first.* The realization of Self is unmerited, as given in the definition of Grace.

◆ ◆ ◆

The key to recognizing the primary blind spot or barrier to freedom and Self-Realization is denoted in this simple statement attributed to one of the great Masters. It is worthwhile to repeat this statement to yourself and continue to reflect on it:

*The pre-supposed existence of a non-existing self
seeks salvation for that non-existent self.*

Even if this statement is understood and seen as a clear exposure of the blind spot, it is unlikely to make a difference for most people, because the non-existent, false identity of the "person" will see it as a useful tool to attain freedom. This is how insidious the mental state of a person is. And the person will express dismay at not experiencing freedom after having understood such a statement, which will further ensure their continued identification as a person.

I am not making references to specific teachers or teachings in this book, so that the reader will take in these words as an expression of the Reality of who and what we are, and the truth that arises primarily from that. It is often the case that the teacher becomes as important as the teaching, or it is not noticed that the truth is actually never other than what you *are,* in essence. I will violate that here because in my view this teacher is the only one that I have come in contact with that is committed to pointing out the dilemma I've described above.

Paul Hedderman is a recovering addict who travels around the world delivering a message to small groups of people who are attracted to his unique understanding. He has not become well-known and has not created a large following or organization. Paul is irreverent in his expression, and his talks are intended to deliver a message with impact. He is not an attractive spiritual leader or teacher, and he depends on donations to survive. He created a website that has a name consistent with his irreverent posture: "Zenbitchslap."

Paul argues that all anyone needs to see is that they are being held hostage by an illusory mental state, one that intercepts all incoming data and uses it to maintain dominance. He claims that he has been ordained to deliver this message, and that it is not a matter of his personal will, but rather, the will of who and what he really is.

I consider Paul's message to be a critical key to Self-Realization, because what he says is that in order to recognize the True Self, one need not *do* anything. What *is* necessary is simply to grasp that the illusory mental state that is dominating one's life has no actual consciousness of it's own, and it must be seen for what it is. When this is seen, one travels lighter. When Paul speaks, he says he is not speaking to who the listeners consider themselves to be, but rather, he is speaking to the actual Self, with the intention that the message will stimulate an expression of Grace from which an awakening can occur.

It is evident that when a person fails to "see" the reality of what and who they are, it can only be because they are looking at it from what they are not. And this is the view of a conditioned "person" who at best can *attempt* to be free, but cannot possibly succeed because the very barrier to freedom *is the identification with this "person" as the self*. Furthermore, if it is seen that freedom is already the case, and that the persistence of the mind continually generating the illusion of self is blocking this, nothing will be more important than to shift attention to and reside as the truth of Self.

This is the essence of the practice of "Self-Enquiry," which is to consistently move attention away from the "selfing" process and toward the Awareness that is always available. By starving the existence of the illusion of a person, which depends on consistent attention, the mental processes that generate the experience of being a person weaken, and at some point the mind reorganizes itself to follow the will of the actual Self. This happens completely upon the Realization of the truth; however, the programming of the mind will continue to appear until it no longer attracts any attention as evidence of a separate self. When attention is moved away from any internal or external object of attention, in the interest of recognizing the Self, attention falls back into its Source.

THE POSSIBILITY

◆ ◆ ◆

If you are interested in the possibility of being fulfilled, happy, and free from psychological and emotional suffering, this book can provide you with insight and offer you specific ways to move forward.

Almost all of humanity is possessed by a mental state that continues to perpetuate suffering and resignation. At some point even the most "successful" people who have been able to manage life and maintain some degree of well-being and security will come to recognize that something is missing. As the body ages it becomes evident that to attempt to control life through material wealth or any other limited means is destined to fail. If there is a possibility to escape from a world that cannot provide true well-being and lasting happiness, this possibility must become the prime focus of one's life.

This is especially relevant to people who seek help from mental health professionals when they are desperate. People who suffer from anxiety, depression, addiction, and dysfunctional relationships with a spouse or immediate family very often have severely limited resources, given the current inadequate and almost nonexistent mental health care available. Considering the limited insurance coverage for such services and the number of people without insurance, most people who are suffering from mental health issues will not receive treatment. This often means that they will ask for medications from their primary care physician to control symptoms, creating new problems of dependency, abuse, and addiction. The use of medications to control symptoms does not address the cause of the symptoms.

Anyone who hears of the possibility for freedom and well-being can pursue it, and if committed, discover a Self that is the very epicenter of being human, a dimension of Consciousness that is free from mental disturbance.

As an experienced psychologist, I can say that even if a person has the opportunity to engage in psychotherapy, it is improbable that it will make a significant difference. This is due to the limitations of conventional approaches.

On the other hand, the possibility for a transformation that can totally eliminate mental health issues *can* be accessed through learning about Self-Realization.There are many teachers of empowerment, mastery, and Self-Realization, and most of them are not part of the professional mental health world. They may be of any occupation and may or may not have a degree. They may appear to be a common person who is not interested in being recognized as a teacher or guide. This is because the spiritual education they offer has no formal certification or degree programs. Such teachers are often called "Masters" because they have realized the possibility of being free from the limited states of mind that are common to almost all of humanity. They are typically considered Spiritual Masters because the teaching and guidance they offer is focused on that which is not physical and is easily ignored.

We are all dying to live. We all want to be fully alive, at ease, and to enjoy life. Dying to live, in a sense, is seeing the possibility of having the life we envision and being open to learning how to realize that possibility. The "dying to live" that will be presented in this book is the easiest death possible because it involves letting go of what is not real and has never actually existed. It involves letting go of an *idea* that has taken on the appearance of being actual and real in itself, rather than being a continuous process of delusion.

It is a dramatic revelation to see that the very person that we have been being—the one that seems so obviously "who we are"—is actually just a belief and does not exist other than in our thinking, which is based on conditioning and an ongoing mental process that generates the illusion of a person. This ongoing process is a very subtle expression of a conclusion we made very early in life. At some point, we concluded that the "I" is an identity and this obscures actual Awareness. We think we see who and what we are as a body, within which there exists a unique, separate identity (or "person") that has a history and specific physical, mental, and emotional qualities.

From that point forward, all that appears follows that conclusion: I was born, I am alive, I act, I feel, I think, I know, etc. Personhood is the domain of considering oneself to be the center of the universe. All that appears, appears to *me;* all that happens, happens to *me.* I am in constant relationship to a world of other people and events that are happening to this "me."

I perceive myself as clearly different than others and often I do not measure up to many of them in terms of my physical appearance, intelligence, accomplishments, and my ability to function. Therefore, I must be constantly learning ways to compensate for my faults and to survive threats to the person I believe I am. This is the process of "becoming a person," and along with the life of a person comes the sense of being a separate and limited "me" in an unpredictable world of other people and situations that threaten the existence of the person as a body and psychological identity.

If we are fortunate enough to be born into relatively comfortable circumstances, we learn to manage our fear and maintain a sense of ourselves as a person. We develop strategies to maintain that comfort while avoiding pain and seeking to improve our lot in the human kingdom. However, there is an underlying angst and concern because this experience of being a person is inherently unstable. The experience of a person in terms of mental, emotional, and physical states is constantly changing. We find ourselves troubled by thoughts, feelings, and physical sensations, and confused about how it is that we produce these uncomfortable and often dysfunctional experiences.

This puts us at odds with ourselves and leaves us with a feeling of being out of control, without seeing how to eliminate the unstable and uncomfortable experiences that negatively affect our life and the lives of those around us. We become neurotic at best; or we develop more serious personality disorders over time.

It could be argued that what we generally consider to be a "normal" person is one who is able to function in acceptable ways even though they may be experiencing unstable emotions and states of mind. If everyone is crazy then no one is crazy. This is the situation, because what passes for sanity includes war, violence, hatred, and a host of dysfunctional behaviors that are fed by commercial enterprises. We all agree that only extremely dysfunctional, dangerous people are actually mentally ill. Nonetheless, the rate of suicide and the widespread use of drugs and alcohol support the fact that people are generally ill at ease. In addition, the growing dependence on ways to distract ourselves from our negative states of mind and emotions further indicates that there is a crisis involving our experience of who we are as highly conditioned, limited, unstable human beings.

If in reality we are not what we have come to believe we are and it is possible to shift to a state of being that is stable and at ease in life, then it behooves us to make this shift the most important goal of our life as a human being.

Dying is an important transformation, and the only real death is the death of the illusion of being a separate, long-lasting entity, living in a body. This book is intended to make that clear, and to reveal the illusion that is commonly understood to be who we are.

THE TEACHING

◆ ◆ ◆

This teaching is consistent with many wisdom traditions that are thousands of years old. It is not presented here in the context of any particular spiritual tradition, because the truth has no particular context, and no specific religious or spiritual path. Yet it can easily be confused with traditional practices and concepts that are simply no longer useful in the current world.

This teaching is a direct path to the realization of the truth of who we are and the reality that this reveals. However, it is imperative to be clear that while seeing who we are is an important step, it is the fulfillment of this possibility that matters. It is only when we are *being* this truth that freedom is realized. And this "being" the truth cannot be realized simply out of an interest or a casual desire, due to our intensive conditioning. We have a firmly established psychological identification with a personality that we have long taken to be who we are. As will be made evident, it is not who we are; who we really are is Awareness itself. Making this key distinction must become the most important purpose of one's life.

◆ ◆ ◆

An Overview of the Teaching

Do not be concerned with understanding all of this now. It will all be explored thoroughly as we progress.

1) Incarnation (birth) is Awareness (spirit, consciousness) manifesting in a limited form in order to experience human life.

2) In order to experience the world and life, an identity named "I" arises that appears to be separate from the world.

3) Attention is directed outward to the world, and thus a human being in the world loses its original sense of itself as Conscious Awareness.

4) The limited, changing, and inherently unstable human identity suffers in the experience of being separate, needy, subject to time and perpetual change, fearful of the unpredictable world, and on a direct trajectory toward death.

5) All attempts to find peace and fulfillment fail in time, and without questioning who we are and what is happening, the human life ends in hope and prayer, or despair and resignation.

6) The question, "Who Am I?" is the beginning of the opportunity life offers to realize the freedom, joy, and eternal fulfillment that is the birthright of all human beings.

7) Paradoxically, the very one who asks "Who am I?" must be seen *not to exist* in order for the truth to be realized and life to be seen as it is.

8) When the self as a separate person is seen not to exist, the Self is recognized, and the separate and limited manifestation of the false identity is seen as merely an appearance, manifested by the mind in time and space.

9) When the person as an actual reality is seen not to exist, it dies (ends), and it is seen that the person never existed other than as an appearance in thought and belief. What was not real and did not actually exist only

dies as an identity, revealing that which has always been real: the Self, or Awareness.

10) Thus, it is seen that death is not real; Awareness is not physical, and has no beginning or end. It is seen that the Self is timeless and eternal and there is liberation from all suffering.

11) It is seen that the human being *is* the Self, and is said to be "*in* the world, but not *of* the world."

12) Conscious Awareness is aware of itself as all there is: One, Boundless Awareness that is at once the field of Awareness as well as all that appears within it.

13) The human life is fulfilled.

IMAGINE

◆ ◆ ◆

I maginationisaninterestingphenomenon. We can conjure up a vision and immediately see images in our mind, as well as potential realities and possibilities. I invite you to use your imagination to visualize the following:

Imagine that your personality has ended. The person that you have been being, that has developed over the years since birth, simply stops. Imagine that the person who has your name, your body, your ways of being, your habits, your views, and your life, just stopped. Notice that the senses still work, and there is an awareness of what is happening.

You can interact with life, but you literally do not experience being a person any longer. If someone were to call your name, you could answer. If you needed to fill out an information form, you would have all the information. When you interacted with your loved ones, you would know how to be with them so they would recognize you. Yet, simultaneously, you would no longer be experiencing this person as who you are.

◆ ◆ ◆

What would that be like, to no longer be a person, yet still present, aware, awake, and free from all of the concerns, negative emotions, bad habits, and fears of the person?

In this *state of consciousness*, you do not have a personality or a past, and you do not have a particular point of view. Although you are still aware of whatever arises in the mind, in this new state of consciousness you are no longer interested in the thoughts, feelings, ways of being, or behaviors that you can now see are not workable and do not express your intentions.
What would that be like?

Consider that you would be free of all that was of concern for the person. There would no longer be a fear of death because the person that you were is now seen to be just an idea you had, or a self-image, so its death would have already occurred. And who you are now is *not* that person, or the body of that person; who you are now is just the *Awareness that was always there but never noticed*. This Awareness has no physical form and although the personality is used to interact with life, it is clear that it is not what you are.

Consider that since you are no longer being a person, the reality that the person experienced is no longer valid. Instead of trying to be happy, for instance, by striving to have the right circumstances that you as a person believe you need in order to be happy, it is simply that you are *already* happy, just being *this present Awareness*, free of all constraints of time, physicality, thought, and emotion. Although these aspects continue, they are no longer happening to *you*, there is simply Awareness and what is happening.

Consider that being Awareness Itself allows you to express the love and gratitude that the person you were always wanted to express, but were afraid to do so.

Consider that Awareness itself has no attachments to anything in life being (or not being) a certain way, so you are free to love it all as it is and be totally engaged in life with abandon.

What if this is really possible? Would you be interested in this transformation? Remember, in one sense you would lose nothing: the thoughts, feelings, and all of the other aspects of your former "personhood" would still be present, and witnessed by "you-as-Awareness-itself," but you would no longer identify with being that person.

It would be like being an actor in a movie of your life. You still have the role to play, but you are able to really enjoy the drama because you are always aware that it is not real. And, you can change the role and behavior of the actor because you are not just the actor, but you are the director and producer as well. What could be a better movie?

What if this is possible? And if it *is* possible, would you want to have that kind of freedom? Freedom from your history and habitual ways of being that cause suffering, freedom from fear and worry about the future and even death itself? Remember, nothing would change except that you would be free from the constraints and limitations of the personality—the person you had always referred to as "I" or "me"— and you would be free to choose to be any way that would be more consistent with what would truly serve you and the people in your world. You would no longer suffer any of the psychological problems or negative habits that the personality had endured for so long.

Would you be interested in this possibility?

Because this possibility is real. As hard as it might be to believe, this possibility is actually available to anyone who is willing to accept that it is real and is willing to have it for themselves.

What if the reason that this possibility is real is that you have *never* actually been the person that you have taken yourself to be? What if the identity has been unconsciously and automatically assumed to be who you are? And, given that our collective reality is one in which almost no one is aware that who they *really* are is not the person that they have always taken themselves to be, you would never question the identity of being a person. This is simply the result of conditioning that has caused us to ignore who we really are. And along with it comes the psychological suffering that is part of that package.

We take on being a body, with ongoing sensations of both pleasure and pain, illness and health. We take on being a personal mind, with a constant stream of thoughts that occur to us as *our* thoughts, many of which torture us. We take on being someone's child that has to meet the expectations of parents, teachers, and the culture. We take on the feelings of being alone, different, afraid, angry, and fortunately, sometimes happy, excited, satisfied, and in love. We take on the constant striving to have more of what we want and less of what we don't want. We take on dealing with the inevitabilities of life: sickness, aging, loss, death, and the unpredictable future. And most of all, we take on the limited experience of being only able to live as an unstable personality, and no matter how much we try, we cannot escape it, so it continues to be a huge burden, generally pervaded by mental and emotional suffering of all kinds.

As a person, you would think that this possibility of transforming one's essential identity is so unrealistic that it could not be so. Many would dismiss it as nonsense. This is quite understandable given the sway of agreement in our world about what is real. It is like believing the earth is flat, then finding out that it isn't. The original assumption changed when the facts revealed that the earth appears to be flat from ground level, but that is not so at all when the point of view is changed. If the life you have been living is in a flat world, then to accept that the world is round would be a major shift in how the world appeared to you. In fact, many rejected the idea when it was first presented.

In the same way, when we look at who we consider ourselves to be, it can be recognized that it is no more real and actual than the world being flat. The only evidence for who you consider yourself to be is the *thought* that you are that. This thought is supported only by inference and not by any actual evidence. For example, you consider your thoughts and your actions to be evidence of a real "you," however this is simply an inference. In fact, you have absolutely no dominion over the thoughts and feelings that arise; if you observe carefully, you will see that you only become aware of thoughts *after* they occur. Therefore, they are not *your* thoughts, they are simply the thoughts that spontaneously arise in the mind. The assumption that they are *your* thoughts is the source of much suffering. Please look and notice that this is the case. You believe that there is a tangible "past" in which you existed, and that the story of your life is evidence of your being real, whereas it is merely composed of images and memories in the mind that you believed to be you.

It is not difficult to recognize that you are not (and never were) a body, even though this is such a common assumption or belief. Is it not the case that you can see the body and be aware of the sensations of the body? Must it not be the case that anything that you can see cannot be what you are? Because if you can see something and be aware of it, it must therefore be at a distance from the you that is seeing it. While this is obviously the case, most people go through life as if they are a body and this brings with it a great deal of suffering. These observations and the conclusions that come with them may seem difficult to accept given the way our conditioning happens. We constantly ignore the evidence, and this is why those who see the truth say that most of humanity lives in a state of ignorance or in a dream.

If life seems to be generally difficult for you, would it not behoove you to give your attention to the possibility offered here?

The evidence for this possibility actually being the truth is very simple. If you were to stop thinking just for a few moments, you would notice that you are still here. That is, without knowing who you are or what is true through the usual process of thinking, you would nevertheless discover that you are still present as Awareness itself, like a baby before it develops language. Even someone who has had total loss of memory and no longer remembers who they are, is still aware, present, and generally able to recognize the environment. If this is the case, then without remembering who you are from the past, you are somehow still here. Therefore, who you are must exist without the identity of being a person, along with a history. If you really look, you will see that this is the truth. And if this is so, then is it not so that what you were asked to imagine is actually already true? Is it not so that who you have believed you are is not actually real and never was?

Even if you don't yet "get" what has been said, if you are willing to accept the possibility being proposed because it resonates with you and you are ready to consider an alternative to the conditioned life given to you as a "person," then just your attention and interest will be sufficient to carry you to the realization of the truth of who you really are.

Are you willing to acknowledge the possibility that there is something you have not previously been aware of that, if given your attention, would totally transform your life and fulfill your deepest desire?

If so, it is only a matter of time, because there is no other possibility for you other than to come to see the truth and be at home as your Self. You will find that no matter what you do or what you think, the only way to peace, fulfillment, happiness and well-being is to be what you already are, which is radically different than who you have always assumed yourself to be.

This book will introduce you to this possibility in more detail and invite you to join the growing numbers of people who have discovered real freedom. This freedom is not freedom *for* you, it is freedom *from* you. Freedom from the you that is not real and has been the primary source of suffering. The invitation is to digest this truth and see if it nurtures you and fulfills on what it has to promise.

THE FULL
CATASTROPHE

◆ ◆ ◆

In order to begin to understand how the common identity for a human being forms, I will provide an overview that describes what happens from birth to being a person as an identity.

We are all born into an already existing world. We inherit the existing collective mind and the existing ways of being that our immediate family, our immediate community, and our immediate culture pass on to us. This state of mind and the ways of being we inherit occur to us as *the way it is:* "Reality." As infants, we have a direct experience of whatever arises in the field of our senses, internally and externally. When we experience discomfort or pain, we cry. When we are comfortable and experience an array of visual, auditory, and physical sensations, we are in wonder, we smile and move about in excited, alive, energetic, and spontaneous gestures. This is the being of a baby.

Eventually the baby learns language, and the world begins to occur conceptually. All things have names and we learn that the names *are* the things. At a certain point the baby relates to the body as "my body," and takes on an identity as a body. The baby's free and spontaneous Awareness that is in direct contact with whatever is occurring transitions to becoming the thinking mind. This is the beginning of the life of the "person." As the baby learns language, the perpetual and familiar "voice in the head" comes into existence and the mental state begins to mediate all information coming into Awareness.

As the person develops a separate identity, feedback information and interpretations of experiences lead to a complex character structure. The mind evolves and judgment and evaluation come into play. The infant person begins to develop a personal mind that is self-conscious. This self-conscious identity compares itself to others and to what is expected, and forms an ego, which is unstable and feels threatened by anything new or anything that appears to challenge its worth or validity.

This process continues and the child becomes more distinct as a personality, with a unique, complex system of reactive, defensive, and aggressive strategies to survive threats to its worth, value, and validity, which are perceived to be threats to its very existence.

As we grow into adulthood, from the view of person or ego, life often occurs as a dangerous and challenging process, and seeking comfort and security becomes a primary motivation for behavior. We try to fit in to find security by identifying with others who share our appearance and our patterns of thoughts, beliefs, and actions. We learn to pretend that we are okay and to seek ways to distract ourselves from the restless discomfort of ongoing change and unpredictability. We learn to deny our anxiety and avoid the growing sense of desperation by distracting ourselves with entertainment, preoccupation with looking good, and being secure with status, accomplishment, wealth, and admiration.

We learn to live inside of relationships that protect us from rejection and the fear of being alone. We join groups, marry, and attempt to build a comfortable lifestyle. And, if we are successful and fortunate enough to live in a place where our daily survival is not an issue, we sit at home watching the suffering and drama of the world on television. We feel that we have succeeded in being the audience to the catastrophe, rather than a victim of it.

None of this is wrong, it is just the passing on of conditioning from generation to generation. It is just Awareness coming into the world of humanity, which requires that it takes on the identity of a body and a person. The specific features that are taken on depends on where one is born and the culture and social realities of that location. Someone born in the United States will be different than someone born in China, Africa, or Russia. The language and customs, and the government and social systems will differ. If one is born into a family where there is abuse and neglect, the psyche of that person will have characteristics that present difficulties. If another is born into a family where there is love and nurturing, that person will reap the benefits of such an environment.

However, no matter where one is born, and no matter what circumstances one is born into, the general reality of being human in a world of turmoil, confusion, ignorance, and suffering will be shared. And the inevitable life in time, identified with a physical body and a psychological identity, will prevail. However, If one awakens to the realization that the full catastrophe, is a result of the identification that has developed in which one considers one's Self to be a person then freedom is possible. When Awareness is considered to be a person, the full catastrophe is happening to the "person." Whereas, when the truth that the person is a construct is realized, and that it is a limited, inherently problematic manifestation of Consciousness, then the possibility of freedom from fear and suffering becomes available.

IGNORANCE

◆ ◆ ◆

There are many forms of ignoring. First, we ignore the truth of time. We tend to live inside a notion of time as an actual reality. We relate to the past and future as though they actually exist, even when we acknowledge that it is obviously not the case. We experience anxiety and apprehension about the future, based on the past. After all, what else can we reference to imagine a future other than the past? And since the truth is that neither the past nor the future exists other than as a concept, when we direct our attention, thoughts, and feelings to the past or future, we are involved with "what is not happening."

◆ ◆ ◆

A primary reason we are so tied to the past and future is because our identity as a person depends on it. We rely on past experiences to maintain a sense of who we are. We have a story, a narrative of our existence that is based on the past. Without this, we could not know who we are. We project this concept of who we are into the future by imagining ourselves in various scenes, either positive or negative. So we are "pretending" that we exist as a person, based on memory and projections. The word pretense is interesting: "an attempt to make something that is not the case appear true." This pretending is not a conscious or intentional process, it is just the way we manage being an identity or person. Another way to consider the pretense is to look at it as an "act." We act as if we know who we are, and as if there is a tangible past and future within which we exist. This is a learned way of being that starts early in life.

◆ ◆ ◆

We are conditioned to reference ourselves with our bodies, our thoughts, and our behaviors. Others in our world interact with us and each other in this context. People refer to each other as a "person"; that is, one who knows who they are based on their name, body, and behavior. This assumption is built into our social contexts very early on. We take on the ideas about who we are without question. This ongoing process that is happening without an awareness of the pretense could be called "selfing." Selfing is the consistent generating of a non-existent self through mental processes.

Selfing produces the appearance of a self, similar to an image of a person on a movie screen. The image is projected and animated by the frames moving through a light, which gives the appearance of a person in a scene. If the film (the past frames and future frames) stops, the light burns through the film and the screen is seen as not moving and free of the images. The Awareness that is the Reality of Being is like the screen. The play of light and imagery on the screen is the dynamic life of the person, the ever-changing movement of life. In terms of reality, the screen and the images moving upon it are actually one. Consciousness is all there is. Although this can be seen as evident, this recognition is difficult to "see" from a conditioned view. Non-duality is the term that is used to mean that there actually are not two. Reality is actually just one happening that appears to be two when the apparent person considers itself separate. If this seems strange or difficult to understand just move on; it will become evident if you continue to contemplate what is presented.

◆ ◆ ◆

Another area where we ignore what the evidence reveals is "thinking." We live our lives with the unquestioned assumption that we are the "thinker." We depend on thinking as a way of knowing what is happening. We relate to thoughts as if they are accurate perceptions of what is happening, rather than as interpretations that are processed through our conditioning and beliefs. When we look at "thinking" in actual experiential terms, we see that what we commonly call thinking is the ongoing experience of having a voice that seems to be inside our heads. This voice provides a non-stop commentary on what is happening, and this commentary involves judgments and evaluations. What is seen is processed based on our conditioning and past experiences. The constant judgments and evaluations provide support for the idea that we are a separate person whose perceptions are accurate about what is happening. This is taken as a position and as a way of validating our views and values. Being right about what is true and real is the way the person survives as a point of view in relationship to all other points of view. This is the source of conflict between people, and ultimately it is the source of war. The way it occurs is "Not only am I right and you are wrong, but your position is in conflict with mine and your position is a threat." Being self-righteous is the source of untold suffering in the world and in our immediate relationships.

Most of us never stop and look at what we are actually experiencing when we are thinking. This is another area of ignorance. The assumption that we are thinking our thoughts is a mistake. This assumption is so embedded in our way of being that it seems difficult to accept that it is not the case. Yet, if we pay close attention to the evidence, it is clear that it cannot be true that we are intentionally and actively thinking thoughts. The most obvious proof of this is that we cannot just stop thinking. If we are doing the thinking, then why is it that we cannot just stop?

Another example of what the evidence reveals is noticing that we do not know what "we think" without first listening within to hear what the voice has said. In other words, we do not generate or create what to think. Many thoughts are negative, troubling thoughts, and many are critical thoughts about ourselves. Some thoughts are fearful, frustrating, or depressing. If we were the source of our thoughts, we would not do that to ourselves. One teacher has said, "If we had a friend who spoke to us the way we speak to ourselves, we would end that relationship." So here again is another example of not "seeing things as they are" or ignoring what is actually happening.

Another illustration of ignorance that causes suffering is expectations. Whenever what happens is different than what we expect, we experience suffering. We feel frustration, anger, conflict, and ultimately hopelessness. This is happening consistently in life, from the small things like the light bulb blowing out in the bathroom when you are late for work, to the big things like being diagnosed with cancer. What we are ignoring here is that life is unpredictable and that expectations set us up for upset. In fact, upset could be defined as an "unfulfilled expectation." Expectations are a function of the notion that what happens should fit the ideas we have about it, that life and other people should fit our "pictures" and when that doesn't happen, it is wrong. Most people don't notice that they operate with the belief that life should not be difficult and uncomfortable at times, and that it should be predictable.

Expectations arise from the very nature of the mind, which is a kind of program that is designed to make sense of the world in ways that support and facilitate the ongoing existence of the person. The mind functions to promote survival of the person by considering all that appears in terms of either gratification for the person or threat to the person. So we assess all that appears and happens in our lives as either desirable and wanted, or undesirable and unwanted. This sets up an interest in having whatever happens be what we want to happen, which translates into what we expect or want.

One simple example is that we want everyone to treat us with respect and positive regard, and so we expect that. When this does not happen, we experience upset and react as if everyone should always treat us the way we want. Or, there is the expectation that we should always be comfortable and not have to be inconvenienced. Therefore we experience upset when we find ourselves in traffic and have to take a detour that will make us late.

Another significant way we ignore reality is the denial of death. We do not allow ourselves to be aware of what Buddhism calls "the truth of impermanence." We keep death out of awareness because we fear not existing. This fear is so intense that it is suppressed and avoided by pretending that it is not going to happen. This is why when death is presented to us by, for example, a terminal diagnosis, we encounter what we have been avoiding (our inevitable demise), and it is a shock. Most people don't want to talk about it, let alone allow themselves to be aware of it consistently. This avoidance of death and the denial of impermanence causes people to live as if they are not going to die. Most people assume that they have endless amounts of time, and they ignore the value of each moment and the value of life itself.

This fear of not existing is an underlying fear of the "person," and if it is seen that this person is not actually real, it follows that that which does not exist cannot die. Until this truth is seen, death remains real and is the end of one's existence. However, when the truth is seen that Awareness Itself is the true Self, it is possible to realize that the body is only a "time body," and the end of the body does not mean that there is an end to Awareness, given that Awareness is not physical. This realization can provide an end to this primal fear that lives in the background for human beings, but only if it is seen that the constructed person is a psychological phenomenon and not an actual reality, meaning that it does not have an inherent existence like Awareness. The letting go of considering ourselves to be a person, and a physical entity, allows us to experience the mystery of our True Nature. It also allows us to let go into life with full abandon, no longer fearing the finality of death.

The most important aspect of allowing ourselves to be aware of death is the possible realization that death is not real. This will be discussed in more detail later because it is a central aspect of the understanding of the truth, and a potential gateway to being fully awake and alive. It will be seen that in reality, we are dying to live. It could be said that to consciously "die" as a person is actually to be born and to be free, to be "in the world yet not of the world." If the "person" is being dreamt, then when we awaken, we find that we are not gone but are actually really here (present) and all that was generated by the unstable life as a person is gone. This is called "peace," and it is the contentment of being at home in life.

 It is essential to understand ignorance and how it contributes to the condition in which we don't "see" the obvious. As the conditioned mind develops we are preoccupied with thinking and with the outer world, so we totally miss the fact of our own Conscious Awareness.

As you continue reading, see if you can just allow yourself to consider what is being presented without feeling the need to determine if it is right or true, and even drop the need to understand it completely. What follows is not intended to convince you of anything. I suggest that if you merely consider what is presented and look into your own experience, you will "see." In some traditions, people who awaken to the truth are called "seers."

We learn to ignore reality. We ignore the truth of life. We ignore the facts. We celebrate birthdays without allowing ourselves to notice that each birthday brings us closer to the death of the body and that this death can come at any time. We look forward to the future because what is happening now never lasts, and seldom fits our expectations. We ignore the truth of change, the inevitability of human life: loss, pain, sickness, old age, and physical death. This ignoring is not recognized as it gradually develops, and it is consistent with a view of life that is delusional and unrealistic. This ignorance is veiled by the collective (un)consciousness. With almost all of humanity sharing this view of life as a separate "person," it appears to be true and real. But this ignoring of reality and living in denial of the truth results in suffering, and a state of mind that is *at odds with what is happening*. It is inherently neurotic, even psychotic in that it is a very limited, unskillful, reactive attempt to live in a world that *actually only exists in the mind*.

The most tragic truth, which at the same time is a blessing, is that suffering is unnecessary.

We believe that we know who we are. For most of us, who we are is not in question. We move through the world with an assumption that we know who we are. However, clear evidence shows that this is a mistake.

Consider the case of Patsy Cannon of Alabama, who was involved in a car accident in 1986 that left her with severe, retrograde amnesia. All of her memories were rendered inaccessible to her. She had no memory of who she was and no memory of any past events.[1] Patsy Cannon had to discover how to speak again with the help of tapes and friends. She had to acquire a completely fresh ensemble of memories to function once more like a normal human being. Even in her dreams, she recalled nothing of her former life. Having been told all about the "old" Patsy Cannon, and having seen photos of herself, she maintained with unshakable conviction: "That person is dead; I am a new person." And it seemed for her, at least, there was no sense of loss.

So this assumption—that we know who we are as if we are actually a unique person that exists in and of itself—is a mistake. If losing our memories would cause us not to know who we are, then it must follow that the only way we *do* know who we are is *by remembering it.* We build upon past experiences to construct a model of who we are and live as if this were "real" in and of itself. Erode memories, and you wear a person away, bit by bit. Erase all memories and you erase the person completely. Most of us ignore the evidence when it comes to who we are. If we paid attention to the evidence, we would ask the most important question a human being can ask, the question that would give us the opportunity to discover the essence of our being: "Who am I?" This question has huge implications. It brings forth the potential of freedom because upon examination it becomes evident that the source of suffering is not "what is happening," *but rather, it is one's belief and assumption that it is happening to "me."* Continue to consider that freedom from suffering is not a matter of freedom *for* you, but rather freedom *from* you.

The illusion of self is worth giving further attention, given that this illusion has been maintained by most of humanity over many centuries. Consider a cinema analogy again: an actor is cast in a movie, practices being the character so that the act appears to be a real person. The actor learns what that person would do and say in situations scripted by the writer and director. There is a story in which the actor will play out a role. When in the role of the character, the actor puts aside or ignores their *real identity* and gets lost in the part. Since the actor knows the truth—that the story and the actor are not real—the actor can enjoy the experience, no matter what misfortune may befall the character. The whole time the actor is in the role, there is a sense of freedom in the background, because they are aware that it is not real.

Now consider that the actor totally forgets that they are acting, and after working on the movie set insists that they *are* the character from the film. The actor would be diagnosed with a severe mental disorder. In the same way, we learn a role and practice being an identity. (And it could be said, we too have a severe mental disorder!) What makes this so complete is that everyone around us has also learned to be an identity playing a role in a story, so there is no "off the set," and it all appears to be real and true. And yet, as was pointed out with the Patsy Cannon case, we can only know who we are by remembering, just like the actor must remember who they are playing, right down to the lines and behaviors. This is the hijack. We take ourselves to be a real, inherently true self when in *actuality we are invested in an empty pretense*. It is no wonder that depression is so common.

What makes this even more difficult is that the brain and mind have been programmed over time to ensure the survival of the (false) identity. This program is a fundamental operation; any interruption or movement away from being the "person" stimulates thoughts and feelings designed to stop the dissolution of the identity, which the brain and mind would relate to as death. This process of moving attention away from the identity as a person can be very challenging and, if not understood, could undermine awakening.

◆ ◆ ◆

Another way to look at the phenomenon of identity is to yet again consider how a movie works. When a movie plays on a screen, what is happening is that a reel of film with separate pictures on it moves in front of a projection light. The film is moving at a fast enough pace so that the individual images appear to move and create a reality, the movie. We can watch the film and identify with what is happening on the screen, and suspend being aware that it is just a movie. In the same way, we learn that we have a future (the film that has yet to pass through the projector) and we learn that we have a past (the film that has already passed) and our relationship between the past and the future creates the illusion that we exist in the present. So in a sense, I *was* here, I *will* be here, and therefore I *am* here. Of course, this all happens constantly and goes unnoticed in terms of it being an illusion: the movie of "me" and my "life."

While life certainly includes "the full catastrophe," as Zorba the Greek termed it, we increase the drama and add suffering to it by taking it all personally; in other words, perceiving life as though it is happening to "me," rather than life just happening. For example, your thoughts mean little to me; they don't seem relevant to me or important because they are not happening to me. But my thoughts are much more important and I experience being affected by them because they are happening to me and they are about me. Another aspect of this personal way of experiencing life is that we give meaning to what is happening and for the most part we don't notice that the meaning we give is not inherently true. A common example of this is the weather. People often consider a rainy day to be negative when in fact it is just raining. The fact that it is raining on *me* and I interpret that to be negative is how the situation becomes "personal."

Although the ignorance phenomenon could easily be a book on its own, this work focuses on what is possible for us in seeing that we are ignoring reality, as well as realizing a way of escaping from the suffering caused by that ignorance.

How is it that humanity has continued to exist in a realm of suffering and so few have escaped? Consider that the agreed-upon "only reality" is based on a materialistic paradigm, and the way that human beings learn to see themselves and the world is dualistic. In other words, there exists a world that is separate from us and that continues on after we die. Dualism means two, the subject and object. This world is materialistic in that it contains matter that exists in a realm that has laws governing this reality, such as gravity and the laws of Newtonian physics. This paradigm is founded in the way things appear and is proven to be accurate through science; thus it is considered the only established reality there is.

From this way of conceiving reality, it makes sense to identify with the body and to think that we die when the body dies. It also makes sense to find it hard to accept that Consciousness is not physical. This is why those who have seen beyond this appearance are considered to be involved in mystical, religious or spiritual pursuits that are not consistent with the prevailing view of reality. We typically agree that what is not in our visual field still exists, although this belief depends on the notion that there is an objective world. Absent the act of seeing, thinking, hearing —in short, Awareness in its myriad aspects—what have we got? We can believe that there's a universe out there even if all living creatures no longer existed, but this idea is merely a thought, and thought requires a thinking organism. Without any organism, what, if anything, is really there?[2]

As Emerson wrote in "Experience," an essay that confronted the facile positivism of his age: "We have learned that we do not see directly, but mediately, and that we have no means of correcting these colored and distorted lenses which we are, or of computing the amount of their errors. Perhaps these subject-lenses have a creative power; perhaps there are no objects." If we use our first person experience as the final word on "reality," all we need to do to test if the world exists outside of our perception is to close our eyes. The discovery of who we are as Awareness Itself, and the first person recognition that Awareness and what appears in it are one and the same offers us an entirely new possibility for experiencing life. Once it is seen that there is no separate person, it becomes possible to recognize that all that is left is what is happening. What is happening is all there is. This experience is all-inclusive and does not deny the dualistic scientific view, but just sees it as a useful convention rather than the totality of Reality. All that is needed to explore the possibility that we are Awareness Itself is to be willing to consider it and use direct observation to recognize it.While it may take time for this non-dual way of experiencing to replace the dualistic, materialistic model, the fulfillment of its expression is always available to those who endeavor to see it directly and live it as the truth. This is the possibility that is being presented here.

[1] Zen Physics, David Darling, HarperCollins, 1996, pg.53

[2] Biocentrism, How life and Consiousness are the keys to Understanding the True Nature of the Universe, Robert Lanza, MD, with Bob Berman, Benbella Books, Dallas, TX 2009

FACING IT

◆ ◆ ◆

To wake up to the truth and stop ignoring reality is to be willing to acknowledge that life as it is typically experienced is not workable or satisfying. This involves a willingness to look at life and be brutally honest as if it were a matter of facts, rather than stories, opinions, beliefs, or limited views.

This can be very difficult because it involves the recognition that what has appeared to be real and true is actually not the case. What brings this into view may be a confrontation with mortality, some significant loss, or a psychological condition such as depression or acute anxiety that totally shatters the ability to maintain any sense of stability. When there is a sense of futility wherein it is seen that this limited, conditioned life is unworkable and can never fulfill the desire for stability and peace, the possibility of awakening increases. This awakening is a matter of seeing the Unconditioned Awareness that has always been present, yet unnoticed. If one gets a glimpse of Awareness, while it may not last, it exposes the potential of freedom and stimulates the desire to realize Awareness as the Ground of Being.

In a sense, facing this confusion of identity is like doing an intervention on yourself, the kind that people do with loved ones who are lost in addiction. For being a personality is a kind of addiction; it is a series of habit patterns that revolve around an endless quest for pleasure, comfort, control, and countless strategies to avoid pain and discomfort. The late Zen Master, Bernie Glassman, once said, "I've managed to rid myself of all my addictions except one; that one I can't seem to give up. I'm still addicted to thinking that I'm Bernie."

Thinking is the addiction in action. Identification with thinking is a blind spot for human beings. Until and unless the person sees they are possessed by the activity of thought and emotion, and that this results in a sense of being trapped, there is no possibility for freedom. When this experience of being stuck is sensed without a vision for freedom, life can become so depressing and futile that the person will even kill that which it considers itself to be—the body—to escape, thus ending the enormous opportunity that life offers. If, on the other hand, the condition of feeling trapped generates the sincere desire to come into contact with the truth, the possibility of freedom becomes available.

When it is seen that there is no experience, situation, or possession that can fulfill the desire to be free and totally open and present to enjoy life, there will arise either resignation or a desperate interest to discover what is possible. The desperate desire to realize freedom is necessary to move through the confusion and mental challenges that come as the bridge to freedom is crossed.

The absolute futility of personhood must be seen if one is to abandon hope. Abandon the hope that if we just keep trying as the person—and constantly striving to change who we are and our circumstances—we will succeed and be happy someday, although had we been paying attention, we would have realized a long time ago that "someday" never seems to arrive.

A dog does not try to be a dog. It does not even know what a dog is. Nor does it need to know what a dog is in order to be what it is.

We have an obsession with identity. We have come into a world of names and labels as a way of knowing who and what everything is, and we've gotten lost in a world of concepts about life, yet we are always one step removed from life itself. But there are no nouns in reality. A tree is not a "thing," it is "happening," and it does not ever exist as the name we call it. In the same way, we are not things: no name can describe us, and there are no "human beings." What *does* exist is occurring in the space of Awareness in which whatever appears is continuously changing, having no name. And, our continued attempts to be what we think we are only result in further suffering. If we were being what we really are and then merely using a name for convenience, to interact in the world, it would not be limiting, it would be an expression of the True Self.

It is our blindness to the Ground of Being that results in restlessness and dependence on constantly generating evidence of our existence. This job of "selfing" is an endless form of the most insidious, energy-draining activity of the mind. Selfing refers to the constant mental activity necessary to maintain the illusion of a consistent identity. The ongoing angst of losing touch with this idea we have of ourselves is the basis of the underlying concern people live with. This is why letting go and just being Awareness often brings forth the fear of non-existing. The identity is facing the unknown, which is feared because it infers an end to security and the ability to navigate in a world that is understood and familiar. This fear of the unknown is generated by the mind. Awareness is and has always been that which knows directly and is free from fear. Turning to the truth is a great relief, for it frees us of the illusions we have constantly been generating to try to keep us secure, and allows us to relax and enjoy life.

HAVING ENOUGH

◆ ◆ ◆

I f one is to look for a way to be free, it is necessary to have had enough of a life that continues to recycle patterns of suffering. One must be willing to consider the possibility that there is something unseen that might make a profound difference in the experience of life. Often when something happens that upsets the seeming stability of life, like a sudden unexpected loss, it causes a person to look for some way to understand what is happening that will provide relief. Or it may be that no matter how much one tries, life continues to be so unstable and unpredictable that everything just seems futile and hopeless.

In some cases, people who feel that they can no longer cope with life and are desperate or even suicidal, have an unexpected awakening that changes the entire way they see life. As people age they often become interested in spiritual matters and begin to see that there is a possibility to be released from the limited ways they have viewed themselves and their lives. Often it is the people who have had a comfortable life that don't recognize the possibility of being free from the tyranny of mental and emotional states, and the ongoing difficulties that follow.

Even after having discovered the freedom and peace that is available when our attention moves from the thinking-based physical identity to the truth of who we are as Awareness, negative mental states will usually return, resulting in confusion. This occurs because there are still aspects of our life as a "person" where there are attachments to states of mind that appear and draw attention. When attention is pulled into a mental/emotional experience, the identity of being the person pops back into place and seems to be real again. This will continue to occur and create confusion until it is seen that Awareness remains as the backdrop for all experience at all times, but is ignored and obscured when the habit of identifying with thoughts occurs. The recognition that this falling back into identifying as the person is an automatic, deeply-ingrained habit caused by brain patterns, allows this confusion to clear over time. It is like turning the power source off for a fan and the blades continue to move for a while.

The most profound attachment is the identification with the body. In fact, the body is considered to be the primary appearance of the person; it is the way we identify ourselves in the world. When we conjure up a memory of ourselves in the past, we see an image of a body. When we imagine ourselves in the future we see an image of a body. When we are asked for identification, we present a picture of the body to show who we are. To let go of this way of identifying ourselves can be a scary experience. Yet at the same time, it is liberating because the body is one of the most uncomfortable ways impermanence is experienced.

As the body ages and degenerates, unless we recognize that we are not the body, there will be suffering. When we are free from this identification and we see that we are that which does not change—Awareness Itself—we can come to accept that the body ages and eventually comes to an end. Even if this form of identification continues, the fact that we know it is not what we are provides a sense of freedom. It is useful to note that if we pay close attention, we can recognize that we are not being in a body when dreaming at night or in a deep sleep. It is also useful to consider that many people have reported "out of body" experiences (OBEs) that have been documented by medical professionals. You can do an experiment where you focus conscious attention on being aware of your entire body, and you will see that the body is within Awareness, rather than Awareness being within the body.

People who are suffering from the attachment to and identification with the body often find it to be possible to let go of that identity and function in very effective ways. This is the case with people who are paralyzed, such as the famous physicist, Stephen Hawking. Clearly his condition did not deter him from functioning as a creative and highly accomplished human being.

When people find themselves in a situation such as Stephen Hawking, or the many other beings who transcended the dire condition they found themselves in, we are seeing the emergence of formless Awareness as the truth of that person. Nick Vujicic is an inspirational speaker. He was born without arms or legs and suffered a difficult childhood. Today he is a well-known, inspiring speaker who has traveled the world addressing thousands of people, encouraging them to have faith in God. Such a transcendence can only be attributed to his realizing that the Self—who he really is—is not a body. It is common in situations like his for the "person" to go through a very disturbing process, often involving suicide attempts. But as most people like Nick share, at some point they have had enough of the self-pity and hopelessness and discover a place within themselves that is happy to be alive.

Most of us will never know what it is like to be deformed or born without arms and legs, and yet most of us will feel dissatisfied, depressed, and hopeless at times. The question is, when will you have had enough of being so small and preoccupied with compulsive negativity? The "person" is inherently self-centered and neurotic. Brain research reports that most people spend nearly half of their waking state or more involved in thoughts about themselves. This is called "the default state." When there is nothing demanding attention in the outer world, attention automatically goes to the wandering mind and the subject is always oneself as a person. This self-centered, wandering mind is what it is to be neurotic, which is a mental state where there is an anxious concern related to oneself.

Thus, if there is going to be a realization of the truth of who you are, it is essential that you are clear that you have had enough of a life that cannot deliver any stable or consistent experience of well-being and happiness. As long as attention and energy is being given to the process of continuously struggling to get life to deliver fulfillment, without noticing the futility of it, ignorance and suffering will persist.

BECOMING A SEEKER

◆ ◆ ◆

In a human life, opportunities appear that present the possibility of freedom. The recognition of these opportunities is a mysterious phenomenon. They can come in many forms, and they spark the beginning of seeking to realize something that seems to resonate in our very being. This may appear as a moment of clarity that follows an experience of deep desperation. Or it may come as a moment of being moved by love for another, or moved by witnessing natural beauty, such as a sunset or a quiet morning after a winter snow. It may arise when we are lost in music, or in the "zone" while running. It appears during experiences with psychedelic substances, and even in states of what is considered mental illness such as manic states of euphoria or even psychosis. Sometimes this contact with the possibility of freedom arises through hearing someone speak who is "awake," or reading a book that points to the truth.

Once contact is made with this possibility, an interest in it may develop into seeking, or else may fall into the background again as involvement with the challenges of life resume. But for many, at some point the interest begins to burn and ignites a passion to recognize and realize what has been merely glimpsed or sensed. This begins a movement toward "the Real."

In the matter of Self-Realization, seeking is actually ignorance-in-action. We are identified with what we are *not* out of ignorance; that is, we are ignoring the obvious Awareness that is ever-present and is the truth of what we are. Then we complicate this by trying to find what we are, *starting from the mistaken premise.* This makes perfect sense to people who are under the assumption that "thinking" is a useful way to move toward the truth. Because we are identified with the mind and the identity of a "person," it would not occur to us to proceed any other way. So it would seem that "Seek and ye shall find" makes sense.

Seeking can become a way of life that never comes to an end. Paradoxically, it is a way the mind unconsciously *avoids* Self-Realization. As long as Self-Realization is seen as something that can happen in the future, the identity or mental state does not have to face extinction, at least not yet. If Self-Realization is seen as an experience that can happen, but has not yet occurred, it will be blocked by this projection into the future. When Self-Realization is understood, one knows that it has always been the case, and we have always been the Self (Awareness).

Seekers have become a very lucrative market. Spiritual teachers have become commercial products. The Internet and the book market have become a platform for spiritual teachers to compete for followers. This feeds into the idea that there is some particular knowledge or special practice or a unique transmission that will produce Self-Realization or Enlightenment. While it may be the case that there are people who can provide supportive pointing and direction, they can do nothing to bring about Self-Realization.

Seeking is a natural aspect of the process of Self-Realization. However, it can become a detour that lasts for a lifetime if the seeker does not realize that it is just a passing phase and that what is being sought cannot be found. In fact, the seeker is the obstacle to discovering that what is sought has never been lost. This is complicated by the fact that many traditions and teachings describe the process of awakening as a "path," and some traditions state that this path may involve multiple lifetimes. If seeking serves its purpose, it will come to an end in as short a time as possible. What there is to be discovered cannot be found but can only be noticed as that which has always been already here as the truth of what we are and what is real.

GIVING UP THE SEARCH

◆ ◆ ◆

Seeking implies that one does not have what is sought. If this is not the case, that is, one *does* have what is being sought, or more specifically, *one is* what is being sought and is unaware of it, then the act of seeking can ensure that what is being sought will never be found. Said another way, if you already are what you seek, then seeking will draw attention away from that. As a famous teacher said, "What you are looking for is what is looking." Seeking is what appears to be appropriate when the "person" tastes the possibility of freedom yet remains ignorant of the fact of non-duality.

Non-duality is the fact that Awareness and what appears in Awareness are not separate. There is no separate self experiencing the world. If that is seen, then whatever is happening in Awareness is all there is. This does not have to be confusing if it is seen that the person is appearing in Awareness rather than the person being aware. It may require some contemplation to see this, but it can be seen. Remember, the person is a psychological construct that appears in thoughts and through collective conditioning.

Seeking is a natural movement toward the truth. It is through seeking that it is eventually seen that the one that is seeking and the process of seeking are obscuring the obvious. Unfortunately, unless this is understood, seeking can go on for a very long time. The mind is identified with the illusion of being a person. Even after Awareness has been noticed, the mind that is identified as a person will attempt to rein in the attention by presenting the thoughts and feelings that have the most meaning and intensity for the person, so as to reinstate "personhood." When this occurs, Awareness is obscured and there is an experience of confusion and frustration that the realization of the actual being or Essential Nature has been lost. This action of the mental state is not the action of a conscious being; it is simply an automatic program doing its job.

The mind and brain operate to ensure the "person's" survival, and therefore thoughts and feelings automatically arise to bring Awareness back into the identification with personhood, because according to the program, if the person does not exist, then death will have occurred. So the mind and brain are actually trying to achieve survival of a person that does not actually exist other than as a mental construct. When thoughts and feelings arise that attract attention, the seeking mode will be reactivated, because it seems as though the realization of the Self has been lost. This oscillation between the Self and the person can be very disturbing and bring into question whether the seeking is a waste of time because it seems as though the experience of Self or Awareness is not consistent, and may bring doubt as to whether there is a Self other than the personality. However, this oscillation is just the survival program stimulated when attention turns away from the thought process and mental states. This registers in the mind as a threat to existence, or a dying process.

If the seeker can maintain a sense of being Awareness as the Essential Self, this oscillation will gradually give way to a fundamental reorientation of Awareness as the Self, and the mind and brain will reorganize in significant ways. The fear-based reactive patterns that have generated all the mental and emotional activity will gradually disappear. This abandonment of specific neural patterns will give way to new ones that will provide a new level of energy that resets the entire body and results in a profound alteration in consciousness that is very pleasant. In time, the mind and body will settle into the new way of being and the energy will balance. It is essential that this period of elation—merely a passing state—not be misinterpreted to be the Essential Self, or there will be another cycle of losing contact with it, dropping back into a person state, and subsequent seeking. Whatever changes, or whatever arises and passes away, is by definition not the ever-present Ground of Awareness, which does not come and go. If the realization of Self is considered to be merely a consistently pleasurable experience, then when that changes, as all experience does, it will seem as though the Self has been lost. In reality, the Self can never be lost. What appears to be lost is only the illusory identity of the person, grasping at pleasant but impermanent mind-states. Yet timeless and ever-present Awareness is even aware of this sense of the person having lost touch with Awareness!

Seeking comes to an end *when it is realized that there is nothing to seek*. When it is seen that the Self is all there is—that Consciousness and that which appears in Consciousness are one and the same—then non-duality is recognized as an unchanging fact. To be more poetic about it, this abiding as Awareness could also be termed Eternal Presence.

NON-DUALITY IS
A FACT

◆ ◆ ◆

Knocking on the door to get inside, the door opens and I find that I am on the inside. -*Rumi*

It is important to emphasize that what is about to be presented is not easily seen or understood by most people, so if it appears confusing or esoteric, that is because it is being seen from the ordinary, conditioned perspective of duality. Duality, meaning two: subject and object. In the case of the self, it refers to "me" as separate from the world. Therefore, I suggest that you simply entertain what is presented and keep the ideas under consideration as you ponder the teachings of Self-Realization. It is somewhat akin to those Magic Eye posters that were a fad for a while. If you look at them long enough, allowing your eyes to blur, you can eventually see images pop into view that were always there, but because your eyes had been focused on the most predominant images, the embedded ones were not seen. When the embedded image suddenly pops into view, it will be appear to be three-dimensional, clear as day, and difficult to understand why it had been invisible only a moment earlier. Even telling you in advance that the image below is a goblet won't help you see it, until you directly *see it for yourself,* which is a perfect metaphor for this entire book.

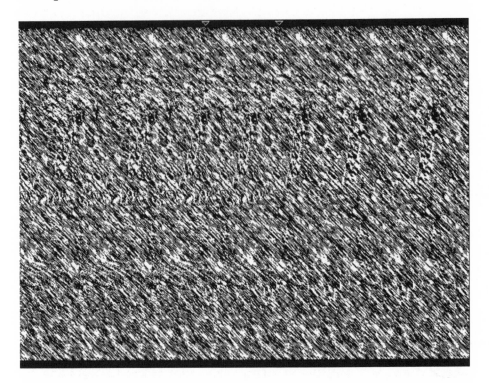

At some point, after learning about non-duality and listening to some of the popular non-dual teachers, I began to "look" into my experience for this aspect of truth. When I eventually did see this reality, what came along with it was a great sense of relief. Because if there is just One, All-Inclusive Reality happening, and therefore no separate, individual self, then it follows that there is no personal "doer," and everything that happens is flowing from intelligent Awareness, which includes all that appears to be happening. Therefore, without a doer, it follows that there is nothing that can be done to realize the True Self. On the one hand, this seems to contradict many of the teachings and practices that speak of a "path" to the realization of truth and freedom. On the other hand, it is consistent with the fact that nothing need be done to realize the Self since we are already this Self.

This may be difficult to grok because we are so conditioned to see the world as outside and our inner experience as inside. However, if consideration is given, it can be seen that this division is merely an interpretation of perception.

It is not that the world is non-dual, rather it is consciousness that is non-dual and the world is none other than consciousness. When this is understood that which appears to be dual, the world that appears to be separate from us, is known to be illusory. This does not mean that we no longer operate or move in the illusory world, what it means is that we no longer take it to be real and we no longer take who we are to be a separate entity.

Try to think of it simply as there is just one happening and all that appears, appears in this one happening. All of what appears separate, the body, the person, all others, all time, all space, all activity are just what is happening. This is the Self, and you are this Self.

This cannot be taken in by the mind. However it can be known directly in the "being" of it. Non-duality is the essence of Self Realization because the Self is just what is happening. You could say the Self is life.

Duality is simply an appearance. Non-dualty is a fact and the truth. To understand this is key to recognizing the Self and seeing that the idea you have of yourself as person is an illusion that is maintained in thought. Just to contemplate this will gradually clear the illusion of the person.

Consider another image. When you look at this image you will see either a rabbit or a duck. There are two images, and yet they are one. This is a way to consider that what appears to be two is actually one.

There is no actual division. Understanding this allows us to recognize that Awareness Itself, as well as all that appears within Awareness, are one and the same. This includes all concepts and ideas about who we are, and all the thoughts, feelings, and sensations that arise. Upon this recognition, it is evident that all that is, is just happening; there are no nouns, only verbs. Who you think you are is happening in Awareness, and is not separate from it. "You" are just a part of what is happening. We think we are aware as if it is one of the characteristics we have as a person. When given our full attention, however, it is obvious that this cannot be the case. Without Awareness, there is no one to be aware. So Awareness is prior to, not after, the idea of being a person. Further, there is no actual reality at all other than Awareness, and Awareness never changes, while that which appears within Awareness is constantly changing. We think we are consistently the same person, but upon paying close attention, we see that we are always changing; our thoughts, feelings, and the physical body are always changing; all that appears—the entire physical universe, including us—is continuously changing. Science has even determined that the cells of our bodies are continuously dying off and being replaced by new ones.

Duality is an expression of Consciousness. The illusion of a separate self is a necessary movement of Consciousness in order to generate experience. There must be the appearance of duality for there to be experience, so that which is non-dual seems to separate itself and appear as two: a person and a world. Duality is necessary to function in this apparent world of "the many." So, the experience of duality and the experience of Awareness-as- True Self are not in conflict. When it is seen and realized that we are Awareness Itself, we continue to function in the world, but we know that this is a convention, rather than the truth. This is why it is said that Consciousness Itself is not an experience, because all experience, good or bad, exists only in the world of time, coming and going—*changing*—whereas *Consciousness Itself is always already present, here and now, every moment.* (Even *this* one!)

Awareness is conscious and aware of itself directly. When we are asked "Are you aware?" and we say "Yes," we are reporting that Awareness is aware of Itself, even though we "think" that we as an individual person is looking at Awareness from the outside and noticing it. This cannot be the case given that there can not be anything "outside Awareness," since it is the non-dual entirety and wholeness of "All that Is." The person is none other than Awareness Itself, and does not actually exist as a separate entity.

David Parrish

The assertion that non-duality is a "fact" is not the way we normally understand what a fact is. We usually depend on collective agreement about what is or is not a fact, and/or on some form of proof that is objective. In this case, it is a matter of seeing non-duality directly as "what's so," or "the way it is." This way of knowing is dependent on being free from our conditioned, habitual view. Seeing Awareness as the actual Self can only occur as a direct perception, and this revelation will not be consistently apparent until it is repeatedly noticed over time and familiarity with it is developed.

To reiterate, the most important aspect of non-duality is the realization that there is no separate, individual, personal self, because this realization frees us from all of the suffering that is inherent in identifying oneself as being the mind/body, not the least of which are the travails of mortality: old age, sickness, and death.

◆ ◆ ◆

Anam Thubten, a Tibetan Buddhist Rinpoche ("Revered Teacher") has summed it up succinctly:

"No self, no problem!"

In the beginning, all of this might be seen merely as an intellectual understanding. However, it must be consistently noticed as life is lived for it to be an ongoing context within which to live. Often after it is seen, but still not really felt or lived in everyday situations, a conclusion is made that it must not be true, that the insight was not accurate in some way. This is a mistake and is caused by the arising of clouded mental states that interrupt the clarity of Awareness.

THE END OF THE SELF AS A PERSON

◆ ◆ ◆

To really get the message that you are not a "person," it is required that you suspend judgment and not arrive at any conclusions until you consider all of what is presented. Then, if you "look" into your own direct experience and contemplate what has been pointed out, you will quite naturally recognize that Awareness has always been the truth of what you are. It is only the mind that is appearing as a person and inferring that thoughts, feelings and actions are being generated by that very same person. The idea that a person is thinking the thoughts is a thought itself. In fact, the person is a thought that is believed into existence. This occurs automatically after many years of repeating the mental process of thinking of yourself as a person and a body.

At the beginning of the quest for happiness and well-being, it is the person, the one that appears to be who you are, that wants to realize the fulfillment of human existence. As one awakens from this false identity, it becomes evident that the one that you consider yourself to be *is actually the barrier to finding what you are searching for.*

The mental and emotional states that occupy attention are a result of the inevitable conditioning that is transmitted by the culture and society into which we are born. We learn that we are a "person" with an individual consciousness that is identified with a body and a narrative or story, and that comprises the whole of our lives. A person, obviously, has a personal experience, including thoughts that consistently infer the existence of the person. As French philosopher Rene Descartes asserted, *cogito ergo sum*: "I think, therefore I am." It is easy to understand that Descartes arrived at this conclusion because it is the same one that most human beings have made, whether consciously or not. The idea that I am a "thinking thing" is accepted as a fact.

What the above paragraph said is that you are not "really" a person; said another way, you are not who you think you are; or, said yet another way, who you think you are *does not actually exist!* It exists only as a thought or concept. This is totally different than actual existence. This "selfing" is a process whereby what happens is continuously being used to infer the existence of a self.

This identity inserts itself in front of experiences as a way of claiming it exists. For example, thoughts are considered "my thoughts." Likewise, if we say "I feel angry," the identity has been added in front of the direct experience of anger, in the form of "I." And we never question this; we never notice that the "I" or "my" of identity has been added to what we are actually experiencing.

When we attempt to realize the truth, sometimes we unwittingly "think" we have recognized our True Nature and we will say "my Awareness," or "I am Awareness." This error effectively eliminates the possibility of actually recognizing the truth of who we are. To correct this we must reverse the process. Rather than the identity recognizing Awareness, Awareness recognizes the identity as not actual or real. *What is real sees what is not real*, rather than what is not real "thinking" it is seeing what is real.

This assertion has profound implications given that all of the problems and conditions that you experience—including the most dreaded ones, like dying—are so difficult to bear because they *happen to you*, and if that you does not exist, all of what appears to happen to you is not actually happening to you. This is a game changer because the assumption that life is happening to you is what makes it all so heavy, difficult, and personal.

As an assertion, this idea that you as a person does not exist is of no real use unless you see that it is true by the authority of your direct experience. In the moment that you see this directly for yourself, and you live from this truth, you are free from suffering. When you are awakened to the truth of who you really are there is an entirely different experience of yourself and your life. This may seem confusing or sound like double-talk. That is because most of us firmly believe that we know who we are, and the idea that this is not true, and that there is a "you that is real" and a "you that is not real" seems to contradict the generally accepted notion of who we are. But the reality of who we are is quite simple when noticed. It can be recognized that who we really are is ordinary Awareness, always present and always available. There is a way of looking at the evidence and a way of looking directly at experience that will allow you to see the truth of yourself and begin to live from that perception.

In my work as a psychologist, the recognition of the truth of who we are and the implications of this have dramatically changed my approach to psychotherapy. The recognition of this fundamental truth has made it possible to work with people with anxiety issues and depression in a very powerful way. If a person is depressed or anxious, rather than help them to sort through irrational thoughts and "solve their problems," it is possible to simply assist them in seeing that who they really are is not the thinker who believes it is anxious or depressed. So rather than an improvement, there can be a total transformation. Depression and anxiety can totally disappear.

This may seem to be unrealistic, and yet it has proved to be true and real in my experience as a therapist. In fact, if a person learns about Self-Enquiry and practices giving attention to, and living as, the awake and aware essence that they really are, they do not need psychotherapy. Because rather than trying to change the person, the process of Self-discovery is about letting go of being a person with problems and living as the actual Self that has always been the truth.

For this realization to occur, the client must maintain an open way of being and be committed to the process of awakening. This can be challenging given that the mind will produce a fear response to this process due to its programming which is designed to ensure the survival of the person. Thus, it is essential to have support to stay on track. The confusion that arises stems from the fact that the thoughts and feelings "appear" to be coming from the person as an actual self. Thoughts like "I am losing control," or "I can never escape this condition" will arise and attract attention. Attention then feeds the thoughts and increases concern, which further increases the thoughts and feelings. As this ramping up of thoughts, feelings, and physical sensations continues it produces a projected perception of who we are that is a distortion.

This is a vicious cycle that often produces chronic anxiety and depression, which in turn feeds the thoughts and feelings, and often results in the person feeling a need to escape the influence of anyone who appears to be aware and is pointing to Awareness. This is because the possibility of Awareness as the True Self threatens the state of mind that has erroneously been considered to be the Self. If this is seen through, and the person stays in the presence of Awareness, a significant shift will begin to occur. When attention becomes attracted to Awareness Itself, rather than what appears in Awareness, then Awareness is accepted as the true identity. This process can be complicated without the support of an awakened guide and/or a community of practitioners engaged in Self-Enquiry.

This teaching is not new, and yet it has remained unavailable to most because it has been obscured by spiritual trappings and religious ideas. In many cultures and spiritual traditions, these teachings of truth have taken on an appearance that was consistent with the mystical flavor of a time when we did not have the psychological or scientific understandings that we have now. Therefore, I avoid references to these religious traditions to make it clear that what is true and real can be seen and realized without such trappings. It is time for us to make these teachings and practices available to all, by speaking in terms that everyone can readily accept and understand.

This discovery and realization is really the key to fulfilling the potential and possibility of being human; it provides stability, clarity, and overall well-being.

Meditation has become a mainstream phenomenon, especially in the West. Mindfulness has become a popular movement that offers the promise of changing the brain and taming the mind. While these practices can have great value, without the distinction between the illusion of self and the actual Self, meditation and mindfulness can perpetuate a life that remains unstable and subject to fluctuations of emotion, states of mind, and the numerous challenges presented by life. When one practices these methods to seek liberation for a person that does not exist, the continued practices bring that non-existing person along and miss the point. For a non-existing entity to seek freedom from itself is a never-ending, impossible journey, *because the very one who is seeking a way out is that which keeps us in bondage,* whether it thinks it's on a spiritual path or not.

Therefore, it is only after realizing the True Self that meditation can be of use, and after the realization of the True Self, meditation is nothing other than the abiding as Awareness, aware of Itself.

While the waking up to the truth of who and what we are can occur at any time, since it has always been the case and is always already present, for most of us waking up and living as this True Self occurs gradually. It begins with making contact with the possibility through glimpses that may arise from the use of mind-expanding drugs, or through contact with a particular teaching, or if in a state of surrender that comes when one is desperate. It may even occur when one experiences states of mind that are considered mental disorders, like bipolar experiences that involve what are considered delusions. When contact is made with the possibility of freedom through some expansive state, the person begins to explore and seek ways and means to experience the ease of life, the freedom of being, and the natural state of contentment, satisfaction and enjoyment that is available.

All of humanity is seeking to realize a state of well-being that is only available when the truth of Self is seen and recognized. People seek security, control, pleasure, and above all, consistent happiness. This seeking usually manifests in behaviors that are consistent with the material world, like desiring money, fame, or power.

When we stop ignoring what is obvious and true and consistently give attention to Awareness Itself, we can begin to be free of the suffering and difficulties of attempting to live as an unstable, ever-changing, fear-based personality.

THE FULFILLMENT

◆ ◆ ◆

When we are born, we leave our full, undivided Awareness, and manifest as an individual, unique, physical form, which evolves into a psychological identity that is considered to be located in the body. Although it is not recognized as this happens, the movement of Awareness into a limited state sets up a profound sense of loss. This loss is perceived as a need to connect to others as an attempt to experience fulfillment and relax the anxiety that is unwittingly being caused by the separation at birth from undivided Awareness. This feeling of angst is constant and causes the existential anxiety that is common to all human beings. Given that it is constant, it is only clearly noticed when it is stimulated by some threat to the limited, vulnerable, and unstable psychological identity. If multiple attempts at fulfilling the void left by this separation from undivided Awareness continue to be frustrated, a feeling of despair and hopelessness sets in that can be called "depression." Or, if there is a constant feeling of concern and apprehension due to the sense of being incomplete, a condition of "general or acute anxiety" arises.

If the person comes upon teachings that point out that the psychological identity and the physical body are limited and unreal, or the person experiences a shock that brings about this recognition, the possibility of ending the sense of being incomplete and unfulfilled may be perceived. After this recognition, if the person continues to notice Awareness as the Source and essence of Being, the limited, unfulfilled experience begins to dissipate. As this happens, the human being fulfills the potential of Being in human form while existing as pure Awareness, which is free from the limits and suffering of the psychological person.

A human being coming into the world has the seed of Awareness, but unless and until there is an awakening into the full recognition and Realization of what the Being is, it will not bloom in this life. When there *is* an awakening, the human being blooms into the "flower" of Realization, and grasps that not only are they Awareness Itself, but all that exists is Awareness. This is the fulfillment of the possibility of Self-Realization.

ON HAVING NO
FUTURE

◆ ◆ ◆

W hile the future is a practical concept, the person relates to it as a reality, just as the person considers itself to be real. When seen clearly, however, the future does not exist other than as a projection or concept. The person projects itself into this non-existent future, and this generates a belief that awakening can occur "someday," and thus the process of attempting to realize the Self naturally follows. When we encounter the possibility of being free and realizing our True Nature, it automatically occurs as "I can be free and I will be free at some point in the future."

The Realization of that which we already are, by definition, can only occur in the present. It is imperative, therefore, to recognize that we have no time to realize the truth. The present moment *is* Reality; it is all there is, and everything that appears in time and space only occurs in the present moment. This is where Awareness exists. This is where all of reality exists, in and as Awareness Itself. In more accurate terms, there is no present without it being related to an imaginary past and future, so it is more accurate to say that Reality is timeless.

◆ ◆ ◆

When this truth is evident, it is clear that there is no need to be concerned about the future. In a practical sense, whatever requires planning will be seen and addressed, and it is understood that what is happening unfolds in accord with a wisdom that is beyond understanding. As this is accepted, it is evident that all is well.

All shall be well, and all shall be well,
and all manner of thing shall be well'"
— *Lady Julian of Norwich*

NO DEATH

◆ ◆ ◆

The fact that death is only relevant to the person is the very essence of why death is such an important point of focus. If it is examined closely it can be seen that death is actually only the death of who we assume that we are. It is the end of the existence of this person and this body that is feared. Thus, death is a prime motivator to seek an alternative, and the good news is that there *is* an alternative. If we are not the body, and what we really are is not subject to that which changes and ultimately perishes, then there is no death for the Self.

This is not understandable from the orientation of a person who relates to life via the senses, which means with a body, but it is possible to let go and be free of this orientation. Awareness does not require an object of awareness to be Awareness. The proof of this is profound: Awareness is aware of itself not as an object "out there, to be aware *of*," but directly as Itself. This is the veil, in a sense, because we are oriented to noticing objects of Awareness through the senses, and it escapes us that Awareness can be aware of Itself. Yet when we experience our Self as Awareness, there is no subject object relationship, and therefore there is no duality. No duality means no person, and therefore no one to die. There is only what is happening. We are Consciousness as well as what appears in Consciousness at the same time. This is the miracle of Self-Realization. In the realm of the Self, death does not exist. There is nothing to die; there is no time, no change.

The identification with the body is the most difficult aspect of the human life to release. After all, incarnation is Awareness orienting Itself in the body to use the senses in order to make contact with life as a human being. And even though we all have "out of body" experiences, such as dreaming, our everyday life is played out as a body, a dynamic form moving in space and time.

It is not necessary to totally break this attachment or this orientation. What is crucial is to be clear that Awareness is not physical and therefore is not the body, so that one's ordinary orientation is seen for what it is. And as a result, one's relationship to the body is different. For example, Awareness, i.e., who we are, does not get sick or have pain, yet the body does get sick and have pain. While the pain and sickness are happening to the body, Awareness does not suffer. It is the person who is attached and identifies as a body that suffers. This does not mean that there is no physical pain; however, the way the Self relates to the pain is much different than the mental and emotional states that prevail when the personality is considered to be the Self. In other words, as many teachers have stated, there is a distinction between pain and suffering. Pain is inevitable, for the body; suffering is an unnecessary phenomenon *we add* to pain, through our misperception of to whom the pain is occurring.

When seen in the light of Awareness, death is an important passage from personhood to Self. If it is seen that when we consider ourselves to be the person there is suffering, it can be concluded that dying as soon as possible would be to awaken to the Self. But this is merely the death of an illusion, not the Self. So in a very real sense, when the illusory self is seen for what it is, *it is no longer considered to have its own existence* and so it comes to an end as a separate self. This death will occur as a natural process when the truth is seen and the person is no longer the center of attention. The death of the body is the end of the senses with which Awareness experienced the world, however Awareness never needed senses to be aware of Itself because it is not phenomenal.

Suicide is a futile attempt on the part of the person to escape from the suffering of the person. It is a mistake in that the actual Self cannot die so the death of the body and the imagined person that inhabited the body changes nothing. Suicide is the most obvious act of confusion. When seen in the light of Awareness, no one dies. The life of the person is an appearance in time that can evolve to the Realization of the Self or pass on without fulfilling its potential.

Although this is not recognized, we actually *want* to die as a person; that is why people hope that there is life after death, so that they can "rest in peace." This life after death is considered to be a spiritual life that is finally free from the suffering of the world. However, what is not seen is that this version of life after death is available now and does not require the death of the body. But, again, and this cannot be stressed enough, this death is a paradox because what is referred to that dies (the person), actually never lived because it is a mental construct, *not an aware entity*. So what dies is simply the idea or belief that who you are was born and will die. When you look directly at what is present in the moment, that which we call Awareness, Consciousness, Isness, or Being, it is seen that there is no beginning nor end to what is here. It is just here, or more accurately, it just "is." This is why who we actually are is often spoken of as the "unborn." The veil of ignorance that hides this is the mental state that is based on the conclusion that there is an "I" that can be aware. When the veil lifts, it is evident that the "I" *is awareness*.

If in reality there is no death, then those who live in ignorance suffer from a great delusion. The dynamic play of Consciousness provides the drama, confusion, and suffering that is the result of

ignorance. All of the horror in the world is of no actual conse-
quence. It is what provides the "bad dream" from which we can
awaken. And yet at the same time, it is within this drama that the
light of Awareness can shine and reveal the truth. What is serious
about the drama is how serious it appears to be. From the view of
the Self, its ever-changing forms are of no concern. A human life
beginning and ending is no more significant than plants and trees
dying and coming to life again. So, dying as the person is awakening to the timeless. As a great teacher said, "You have one life, and
it is forever."

THE MIND

◆ ◆ ◆

The mind is a concept that is used to distinguish a kind of mental space within which thoughts and images arise. It is not an actual place or an aspect of the brain. Rather, it is where the identity is formed and generated moment to moment through mental processes. This identity is a fixed notion of an "I" that is maintained by inference alone. When this identity believes itself to be "a real and separate, phenomenal being," it considers the mind to be "*my* mind." The identity identifies with the mind as itself, so that all thoughts that arise are considered to be "*my* thoughts." Likewise, feelings and physical sensations that arise in the mind are considered to be "*my* feelings and sensations." Thus, the mind becomes synonymous with the identity.

When the possibility of Awareness being the truth of who and what we are arises, the mind reacts and resists, because this new possibility threatens the entire matrix of reality that it has developed through conditioning and past experiences. The mind is no longer seen to be the identity in the sense of it being "my mind" or "me," as in "me" thinking, but is now reduced to being only one, very limited aspect of the vastness of Awareness.

In a sense, Awareness occurs to the programming of the mind as an invader that threatens its very existence as the seat of the self. This is a very precarious situation because the familiar and entrenched identity established in the mind can and *does* sense itself to be Awareness, and thus becomes at odds with itself. This is seen in the previous statement, "A presupposed, non-existing self wants salvation for that same non-existing self." This is when the identity becomes a "seeker," and for many this feels over-whelming. Fear arises and it may appear that there is no way to be in existence as Awareness, which brings up the fear of death. Unless this fear and overwhelm is understood to be evidence of a movement toward Self-Realization, the "person" may deny the possibility and retreat to the safety of the known.

If it is seen that this fear and overwhelm is not a threat to the truth of Awareness, then the movement toward Self-Realization will continue. However, depending on the maturity of the per-son, there may be a very uncomfortable period of "mind attacks" in which the mind presents the person with thoughts and feelings that stimulate fear, doubt, and confusion. If these attacks are not understood for what they are, they could continue and result in severe anxiety, panic, and depression. This is why it is so import-ant to have a guide who is familiar with the process who can provide support and point out that these problematic mental/ emotional states can be brought to an end by letting go of iden-tifying oneself solely as the mind and discovering the freedom of Awareness.

If there is a significant attachment to being the person, and a fear that to *not* be the person will result in a loss of what are considered important beliefs, relationships, positions in life, se-curity, or certainty about how to be in the world, this process could become an ongoing purgatory, an experience of being stuck between two worlds and not able to live in either one. Even if this occurs, it remains true that if it is seen that it is the ongoing iden-tification as a person that is causing the confusion, freedom can be realized. The difficulty is that if the confusion is not seen, then the suffering must continue until the reality of what is happening is recognized. This is the insidious nature of the mind and the projections of the mind. Such blindness is a function of the person not "seeing" that they are attempting to be free while remaining "the person," which is the very thing from which they are seeking freedom. In other words, they have not really seen the truth of who they are, but have only known of it as a mental concept and have mistaken the concept for reality.

It is interesting to note that "knowledge," as it relates to being stuck in the orientation as "the person," is detrimental. Knowledge can actually be the barrier to Self-Realization. When a person thinks they "know," there is no longer a possibility of discovering. The subject is closed. This is the state of most of humanity: they "know" who they are, and they also think they know what Reality is. There are "experts" who assert that what is real can only be known through the scientific method. There are also experts who argue that a human being is merely a phenomenal entity, a physical person. They believe that Awareness is produced by the brain when the complexity of the brain reaches a specific point of development. These experts state that once they have more of an understanding of how the brain does this, they will be able to prove this theory.

When it is seen that knowledge is a limited mental process that involves naming and fitting whatever appears into a system, it is also understood that Reality is beyond what can be named or mapped. Conscious Awareness cannot be measured or controlled. The direct awareness of Awareness is not a process of knowing. Awareness cannot be known. It cannot be fit into any system of thought. Awareness can never be an object that can be located in a particular time or place. It cannot be seen, and yet seeing is its nature. The recognition of Awareness as the truth of what we are is a matter of letting go of all mentations and being empty. When this is seen, being empty is recognized as Awareness itself.

A key aspect of maturity is to be aware of the mind as the mind, in the sense that what appears in thought is not automatically regarded as true or real, but is seen as the mind producing interpretations, reactions, and narratives about what is happening. When this maturity is realized, the mind begins to be in service to the Self rather than the person being controlled by the mind.

WHY PRACTICE?

◆ ◆ ◆

Practice is the ongoing process of noticing the habit and tendency to identify with thoughts and mental states. It is necessary to practice in order to establish in a different experience of being. The existing habit patterns that produce a consistent experience of ourselves as a psychological construct —commonly called a person or personality—are recorded in the brain and play out in our minds from moment to moment. Without Awareness of this, we are subject to what seems to be a reality in which we are a "person" that exists in time, has free will, and uses thinking as a way of relating to life. In order to escape this limited, unstable, finite existence, we need to awaken to what is actually happening and begin to attend to the truth of what we are. It must be seen that the person is not an inherent reality, that the person does not exist outside of the ideas and thoughts that infer a person. Whereas, *Awareness is actual, real, and inherently exists prior to and without thought.*

The identity as a person is nowhere to be found outside of the supposition based on indirect evidence. We consider the person to be what we are because we consider the thoughts that arise in Awareness to be *our* thoughts; therefore, thinking implies a thinker. However, upon examination it can be seen that there is no evidence of a person that exists of itself outside of thinking.This recognition is the essential beginning of an inquiry to establish what we actually are. This is not merely a philosophical theory; rather, it is directly and experientially evident upon examination that there is truly no actual "person" apart from the *idea* of a person that is constantly maintained and reinforced by memory and an agreed-upon, collective reality.

If this is seen, it opens up the inquiry because of the presence of "I am," which is the direct experience of a be-ing in existence. Here the "I" refers to Awareness, rather than a "person" or a seemingly personal thought. This is a direct, obvious experience. Therefore, if the person is a learned concept, what then is the truth of that which we call "I"? This "I" must exist outside of thoughts and concepts, since it is able to be aware *of* thoughts and concepts. In the identical way, if you are aware of a car, you intuitively know that you are not the car. The same is true if you are aware of thinking. The thoughts cannot be you. Hence, Awareness exists prior to the idea of a person. It starts to become apparent upon looking that this Awareness that we call "I" is very different from what we have previously identified ourselves to be. Awareness is always present and is the Ground of Being from which all appearances arise. As this is seen, attention moves from thoughts to Awareness itself. And although this can be seen, the insight will be lost when attention is again taken over by thoughts, because *thoughts are grounded in a system of belief that has established us as a person.* Therefore, we have to *practice* attending to Awareness to break the habit of considering ourselves to be a person limited by conditioning, thinking, and emotional reactions. This is a matter of waking up from a very powerful hypnotic state.

Spiritual masters have said that to practice attending to the direct experience of Awareness as the reality of our existence will, in time, establish Awareness as our Ground of Being. This practice can be challenging because the mind is conditioned to identify the person as the "self." And the mind's fundamental programming is to ensure the survival of this finite self. This deeply-embedded program will only change if, over time, attention is directed away from the mind until it adjusts to the fact that the real Self *is* Awareness.

This occurs over time as the mind and attention succeed at dropping the illusion of a "person." And it is noticed that without the person, Awareness remains. During this period there may be an experience of dying, of the person coming to an end, and this may stimulate fear. Since we identify with being a person inhabiting a body, death is the end of this phenomenological and psychological existence, and the birth of Self as Awareness remains as the truth. The body remains a useful vehicle for transportation in the world, and the person remains as a tool for the expression of Awareness, rather than as an end in itself.

This practice of attending to Awareness amounts to Awareness being aware of Itself, because the "person" is a very limited expression of awareness. Only Awareness is completely aware, and it is aware of Itself. This is one way of defining enlightenment. When it is practiced, there is a shift from being concerned, anxious, and self-conscious, to a sense of being peaceful and content, and enjoying a natural, effortless way of knowing and acting. The "person" is also the Self made manifest in a finite form, with a point of view and a relationship to a finite world. This is necessary for there to be an "experience" of the finite world, however it is the fulfillment of the human experience to realize Awareness as its Source. When this is recognized, it is seen that Awareness *and what appears within* Awareness, including the image of a person, are *One;* Reality is non-dual, i.e., "not two." So there is in truth no subject and object, no objective material world, but rather, just Conscious Awareness.

Again, as previously stated, it is often reported that these experiences of being awake, aware, and at home with life come to an end when the mind presents thoughts and feelings that pull attention and bring Awareness back into a mental state. If this is not understood it can be very disturbing and result in an unstable experience that stirs up fear and confusion. As this process is seen from Awareness, the mental states no longer attract attention, and diminish. It is discovered that what is not in the light of attention is actually not in existence. For example, have you ever had a painful physical condition that was dominating your consciousness every waking moment? And then something very interesting to you demanded your full attention for 30 minutes? Afterward, you suddenly realize that for those 30 minutes, you had no pain! It literally didn't exist because your attention was elsewhere.

As attention is consistently directed to Awareness, the mental states and the construct of a person are starved of energy. In time, Awareness is again recognized as the "seat of Being," and the person begins to be a conscious expression of Awareness. In fact, Awareness is constant and is never actually interested in, nor distracted from, what the person is experiencing; it is simply seen as what appears to be happening when the mind presents delusions. When Awareness is recognized as the Self, it no longer matters that thoughts or feelings arise. All of it is seen as the passing play of Consciousness in the field of appearances.

Language and thought are dualistic, so until Awareness is established as a consistent Ground of Being, there remains a tendency to fall into a dualistic view. This can be seen when we consider the common use of the word "I" in performing actions, as in: I think, I eat, I work, I sleep, etc. But in Awareness there is no actor, just Awareness of what is happening, with no personal "I" doing it. There are no pronouns, only verbs. Thinking and eating and working are occurring, but there is no "I" performing those actions. Actually nothing has happened because there is no past. Nothing will happen because there is no future. All mental activities that produce these concepts are just what is happening *now*. Personhood is seen as a mental activity rather than the subject of experience. In Awareness, nothing is happening to the person, and there is a sense of freedom from all psychological conditions.

Neuroscientists say that we are *always* practicing. We are unwittingly practicing being a person, with the view of a person, and the thoughts and feeling states of a person, as we continue to repeat these experiences. By repeating these thoughts, feelings, and actions as an expression of a person, we are firing the neurons in the brain that maintain the matrix of a person. The brain and the mental states that arise are combined with the habit of continuously attending to thoughts and feelings as meaningful and relevant to the person. Practice is the process of reorienting and reprogramming the brain and mind to connect with what is actual and be established in the truth of what we are.

This process can be very challenging and yet the challenge itself is necessary and important. It is imperative that the actual Self recognize the illusion of the person and not give attention to the thoughts and feelings that arise from this state of personhood that continue to validate it as the "real" identity. *It is important to be aware of the fact that the person (as a finite appearance) continues in an appropriate relationship to its Source, rather than in isolation as a finite, limited, illusory identity.*

The process of transformation appears to involve change. Change is a constant in life, however this particular appearance of change is unique in that it is the fulfillment of the potential of Conscious Awareness. Transformation is *not* change in the sense that the Self has always been the Self and this Self does not change. Such is the paradox of truth. So, when the Self is Realized, the *person changes* in many significant and profound ways, and yet at the same time nothing has changed since the Self remains the same.

THE VALUE OF
SUFFERING

◆ ◆ ◆

Suffering is useful as a motivator for waking up and realizing the truth because in truth there is no suffering. Suffering is inherent to being a separate person living in a world that is threatening. In order for there to be suffering there must be a sufferer. Human suffering is a matter of being at odds with life, with other people, with physical sensations (pain), with time, and with thoughts and feelings. Being at odds with the way it is, is the condition of the mind of a person.

A personal mind is a mind that is judging and evaluating all that appears. A personal mind is a mind that is related to a brain that is conditioned to seek pleasure and avoid pain. Almost all human beings are totally identified with the mind. They consider thoughts and feelings to be their thoughts and feelings. So, it is the person who thinks "I don't like this." "I don't want this." "This shouldn't be happening." "I can't take this." "I want this." "I like this." "I don't want this to end." It has been said that the source of human suffering is desire. This simply means that the way it is, is not ok, so I desire it to be different.

The key to suffering is the existence of a phantom self. The sufferer is the identity that exists as a state of mind. Meaning that the idea of an "I," or a "me," exists as a mental state that has no actual reality. Suffering cannot exist without a sufferer. And since the sufferer does not actually exist, suffering does not actually exist.

So to end suffering, see the truth and be free.

This is not easy because the mind and the brain continue to produce the illusion of there being a person who exists in a physical body. This pattern of thinking, feeling, and sensing as a person is so engrained in the way it occurs for us that for many, what has been said here will appear confusing or unrealistic. Even though the evidence is irrefutable.

In the case of physical pain, for instance, people typically argue that it is unrealistic to simply say that the suffering will end if they realize that who they are does not suffer, or that suffering does not actually exist. This is understandable given the resistance and intensity of the experience of physical pain. What is not recognized is that physical pain is a part of the existence of a physical body. Suffering is distinct from physical pain. Suffering is the experience of pain as it occurs to a person. So, it is not the pain, it is that the pain is happening to "me" that is the source of the suffering. For people with physical pain this is very difficult to "get" because the they are so identified with the pain, as in: "my pain." This view is not meant to be insensitive to people suffering with acute or chronic pain. And it does not mean that we shouldn't take appropriate actions to control or eliminate pain; only to note that it is different from the suffering that is added to the discomfort of pain. In reality, if one were to be free of the identification of being a person and a body, pain would be more of a pure sensation rather than the state of mental and emotional suffering that usually accompanies it.

Emotional suffering is similar. In the case of depression or anxiety, it is the person who is experiencing these states that suffers. The actual Self does not experience depression or anxiety. In fact, the actual Self does not experience anything. The actual Self is Awareness of what appears, or to be more precise, it is what is happening itself. In the truest sense, there is only what is happening, and this includes everything that occurs in the body and mind and external circumstances, and it is non-dual. Again, this is difficult for most people to grok because depressed or anxious people are very identified with the personality. In fact, it is the preoccupation with the experience of the person that produces the depression or anxiety, which are states that arise from concern about being a person in a threatening world that appears to be unpredictable and uncontrollable.

Suffering is very valuable as a motivation for seeking relief from negative states of mind and the life lived in personhood. The despair that is produced by suffering can bring one to a critical point that can lead to the revelation of the true Self. In many cases, when someone commits suicide it is because they are desperate to escape the states of mind and the emotions inherent to being a person. In some cases, this crisis of identity can result in a breakthrough to recognizing the freedom of Awareness itself. In other cases, the person is so cut off by their preoccupation with negative thoughts and feelings and a hopeless view of life and the future that they fail to recognize the possibility of freedom that is always available and they follow through with destroying the body (suicide).

If the person views human suffering as inevitable and believes that the suffering is being produced by uncontrollable forces like pain, a set of life circumstances, or brain chemistry, then they are locked into a world in which there is no possibility of relief. It is the failure to realize that the identity as a person is the actual source of suffering that has it appear hopeless.

There is a clear relationship between suffering and awakening to the truth of Self. In other words, the more it seems that life is not what it should be, the more suffering there is. People who have success and fame often end up suicidal because they discover that they are not happier because of the money or fame and there do not appear to be any other options. In fact, they are often more stressed and unhappy dealing with trying to maintain fame and protect their money. It is important to realize that temporary gratification and short-lived pleasures never last. What we are all seeking for is something that *will* last, something that does not keep changing, something that is stable. Awareness is all of this, however it cannot be found because it has always been present, albeit unnoticed.

The cosmic joke is that it is all just an illusion. There is no solution to a problem that does not exist. And yet the appearance of a problem appears so real that those who are suffering argue that it is cruel to suggest that there is no problem. This is where those who are suffering need to have faith, and trust that the truth is freedom. If anyone who is suffering is willing to be open to the possibility that freedom from suffering is possible and is willing to stay in the process of "looking", there will be revelations and there will be a release from the bondage of ignorance. This must be so because there is nothing other than the truth. This is the promise of all Sages, Saints, and Masters.

THE BIG QUESTIONS

◆ ◆ ◆

I f Awareness is the truth of who we are, why is it that over thousands of years so few human beings have seen and realized this, especially given the suffering and profound consequences of ignorance?

In regard to the history and evolution of human beings, we tend to consider thousands of years to be a long time. This is a very limited perspective. From a larger view, we could see human evolution to be in its very early stages. If human evolution is evaluated based on the development of technology and science, it may seem that there has been dramatic movement forward. However, if human evolution is evaluated based on our behavior, it is clear that we have not evolved very much at all, and in many ways we have regressed. Our destructive tendencies have advanced to the point where we can destroy the planet much more efficiently and quickly than in previous generations, and we have also become more isolated as individuals and more ego-oriented than those in the past. Material possessions, our appearance, and our many distractions have become more important than ever. At the same time, psychological well-being has deteriorated. War, nationalism, suicide, homicide, and addictions of all sorts have become common aspects of daily life. These forms of suffering may be part of a down cycle of evolution and may stimulate a new movement toward sanity and well-being on a massive scale. Or, humanity may be facing extinction. If so, the mystery of Awareness-Self-God will continue, perhaps as an entirely new universe.

Another aspect of the fact that so few awaken is that the illusion of reality—particularly the illusion of a separate, consistent person—is very persistent and seemingly actual. It has the power of agreement. For most human beings, reality is a function of agreement. Not only is the illusion of a separate person seemingly real, but humanity as a whole is in agreement about it, that the "person" is real and is the truth of who/what we are. This collective agreement creates a perception that occurs as an absolute truth. The passing on of this illusory truth occurs at a very early age, and comes with language and the power of conditioning and socialization.

Early conditioning programs the brain to identify who we are as a body, a thinker, an emotional being, and the actor in our story, and these neural patterns are replayed millions of times over many years. Information that is counter to this programming is commonly ignored or seen as unrealistic, and the conditioned brain and mind will react to such information as being either threatening or nonsensical.

Still another reason for this ignorance is that most people accept what *appears* real to be what *is* real. Prior to it being common knowledge that the earth is round, people believed it to be flat, because it appeared that way from ground level, and everyone agreed to that conclusion, making it a "fact." Likewise, Awareness cannot be seen, so it is easy to ignore and consider it not to be real, which is interesting given that it is the essence of existence for every human being. This is further complicated by the fact that science ignores Consciousness, for the most part, because it has no way to measure it or prove that it exists.

And why is it that even people who come in contact with these teachings nevertheless struggle to come to any consistent state of Being-as-Awareness?

Because the one who struggles can only be the person.

In other words, as long as a person struggles to realize the Self, they are operating from the state of personhood. Just the idea that it is possible to be anything other than the Self will ensure the continued existence of the person. When it is seen that Awareness-as-Self remains the truth even when the person is in the forefront, dominating our attention, the struggle will come to an end of itself. This is consistent with the truth that the "person" *is* the Self, manifesting as a separate being, in a body, so there is never really any being in existence other than the Self. The mind will continue to present person-thoughts, person-feelings, person-memories, and person-ways of being, however when the Self is established as the truth, these thoughts, feelings, memories, and ways of being are not in conflict with the Self.

What is it that allows for a consistent state of being Awareness? Or, said another way: What is the experience that a Realized Being is having in regard to thoughts and emotions such that they are no longer suffering or caught in reactivity? When thoughts and feelings arise and they are no longer taken to be inherently true, they don't pull attention from the seat of awareness. It is the thought that I am the one who suffers, I am depressed, I am angry, etc., when taken to be not just a thought but the unquestioned truth, that brings the suffering world of the person back to the foreground of our attention. The Aware Being is naturally discerning all that appears, and sees what is not real without effort. Awareness has clarity and simply does not identify with what appears.

Awareness needs nothing to be consistent, as it is the only consistent reality. The Self is not an experience that the person *has*, it is life itself, as it is already happening. It is the recognition that Awareness is all that exists, and the person is but another limited and changing appearance and passing aspect of Awareness, rather than a separate, independent entity.

When the Self is Realized, nothing changes and everything is different.

What is different is the view of what appears, and therefore the relationship to what appears is different. When what occurs is seen from the view of a Realized Self, it is seen as it actually is. For example, when someone is meditating and a dog starts to bark, it occurs to a Realized Self as a sound and it has no effect on the meditation. For someone who is unrealized as the Self, it is likely to occur as a distraction (an interpretation of the sound) and as such interferes with the meditation.

The Kingdom of Heaven is not other than the world as it is. The same world that is seen as full of suffering and tragedy appears to the Awakened Being as Heaven. While this may seem difficult to imagine, it is a matter of seeing all human beings as Awareness in the process of awakening. All suffering is seen as an appearance, a play of Consciousness without real consequences. This is what is meant by the quote from *A Course in Miracles* previously mentioned: "Nothing real can be threatened. Nothing unreal exists. Herein lies the peace of God."

To the Self, all that appears is not an objective reality, therefore it is seen differently because its Source is no longer the person or the programmed brain, but rather is Awareness, free from ignorance and distortion. The joy of Being Itself is recognized. The God that is appearing in the play of form is seen to be love itself.

WHAT IF I DON'T
GET IT?

◆ ◆ ◆

This is an important question, because most people will not get it in such a way that they will at long last *be awareness* itself, and thus no longer dwell in the limited and mortal state of personhood. Those for whom the pointings resonate, excite, generate interest, or provide a glimpse, there will be an opening of a new realm of possibility that can herald the beginning of a new life. This new possibility for being will become available and the process of reorientation will commence. This is the point when a teacher or guide can be useful because the mind is insidious, and can easily produce confusion, thoughts and feelings that again pull one's attention into the state of being the "person."

One way to look at this is to ask, "Who is it that is not getting it?" If who it is that is not getting it is the one who is identified with thinking, then the awareness of that itself will reveal that one's attention has been drawn to the state of mind that generates the very person who is not getting it. The "person" cannot "see" awareness because the "person" is appearing in awareness as a thought or memory, and is not real (actual). This can be difficult to grasp, but it is worth giving it attention and staying with it over time until it is seen clearly. A knife cannot cut itself. A scale cannot weigh itself. An eye cannot see itself.

In a very real sense, it is not possible *not* to get it, because you *are* it. The idea that there is something to get, or some particular experience that will serve as evidence that you got it, is itself the problem. In actuality, there is nothing to get because you already are what you are, so just the thought that there is something to get engenders a futile and potentially endless quest for who and what you already are and have been all along.

If you are asked, "What do you need to do in order to be reading this right now?", what is the answer? Are you not already reading this? Therefore the answer must be "nothing." In the same way, if you are asked, "What do you need to do in order to be what you already are?", the only real answer is also "nothing." The only way you can be derailed from being what you are is to believe that you could be other than what you are. If you believe that you are a "person" and this is real, then you will be in the world of the "person," and thus subject to the states of mind that come with that identification. States of mind such as fear, anger, frustration, and confusion. No state of mind or emotional state can threaten awareness, because awareness does not identify with what appears *within awareness*. What appears in awareness simply arises and passes. When what appears seems to be happening to a "person" it is resisted and can continue to persist and become a mental condition or disorder. Awareness is the unchanging field that contains all appearances. The chalkboard does not become what is written on it. Water does not take on the form of what moves within it. Space is not affected by what happens in it. The movie screen does not change when images appear on it. Please give some attention and reflect on these statements so that you can "see" what is being presented for yourself and confirm the truth by your own authority.

The only requirement for getting this is that one cease to auto-matically accept as valid whatever the mind presents. The so-called "person" is merely a state of mind that one takes to be real and valid, so to recognize this, and thus not use the mind as a ref-erence for Self, leaves the truth to be seen.

There is a story of two Zen monks looking at a flag blowing in the wind. A master walks by and asks, "Is the flag moving or is the wind moving" One monk says it is the flag that is moving. The other corrects him and says it is the wind moving. A master points out that it is the mind moving. *The person is a movement of the mind.*

Most human beings are so identified with the mind that they pro-ject mental movements as external realities, like the Zen monks. It is important to recognize that what occurs as the world occurs in the mind and it is different for everyone. There are about eight billion people on the one planet who are seeing eight billion different worlds (world meaning the reality being perceived.) The recognition of this is seen from that which is not different, which is the awareness it Self.

"Most human beings are so identified with the mind that they project mental movements as realities. For example, we have thoughts about who we are which are mental movements, and we consider them to refer to something that is real. When we give attention to this it is possible to see that the idea of who we are is not in existence anywhere but in the mind. When we are upset with someone we are close to, we have "mental movements" i.e. thoughts, negative memories, negative visions of the future that portray the person as a threat, as someone who is against us. In actuality none of this is consistent with what is happening. The person may have simply looked at you in a way that triggered a reaction, or maybe they didn't respond when you spoke. So, it is important to "see" and understand that mental movements, meaning thoughts, images, memories, or fantasies are interpret-ations and are subject to judgments and evaluations that are im-posed upon what is happening.

In order to emerge from the misery of the inconsistent and un-reliable, ever-changing life of a "person," it is necessary to break the spell of the collective culture of ignorance that pervades hu-manity. It requires that the realization of the Self be the most important endeavor in life. Only for those who see that this is the true purpose of life can such a challenge be taken on. This does not mean that it is necessary to withdraw from a typical life; in fact, when the truth is recognized, it becomes obvious that life is consistently presenting opportunities to confirm the truth. For example, when something happens and there is upset it indi-cates that what is happening should not be happening, and there is suffering. The authentic (real or actual) Self, which is simply aware does not reject what is happening, so this can be seen as an indication that the identification as a "person" is at play. So, prior to awakening upsets were seen to be caused by what happened, now upsets can be seen to be caused by the confusion of identify-ing as a person with expectations that result in upsets. Therefore life situations challenge the awakened to continue to confirm the truth. It is seen that all states of mind are in service to Self-Realization in that until mental states no longer have the power to direct and control attention, realization is incomplete. Every-thing that appears in the ever-changing dynamic that life is, can be used as a reminder to stay seated in the awareness that never changes.

Can you take the stand that no matter what arises in the domain of thoughts, feelings, and sensations, you remain resolved to ful-fill on what is possible? What is possible is freedom from the suffering that is common to most human beings. This suffering is caused by the unexamined limited psychological identity that is given by conditioning (being a person that is a separate self existing in time.) This conditioning is not a bad thing, it is simply the process of being in a human state, however this state is limited and if the potential of a human being is fulfilled there will be another stage of life in which the human being will recognize awareness as the authentic ground of being that has the life of the person be seen as a relative truth rather than the absolute truth. This awakening to being aware of what we are as awareness it Self, transcends the relative limited existence of a person. Awareness exists only in the present so time is not real, and this awareness is not a separate physical body or person, but rather is unchanging and the same across all beings. This awareness has no suffering because it has no expectations it simply is present to whatever appears. And finally this awareness reveals that death is not real because for death to be real the awareness would have to have a beginning and exist in time. Therefore while the body is a time body and will pass, the awareness was not born and cannot die. Only the concept of being a person dies. If you give it consideration is it not so that it is the you, that you consider yourself to be that is afraid of death. That you was never actually born, it was invented so it cannot die because it actually never existed other than as a state of mind.

Most of humanity is resigned to the limited life of being a person. Can you move away from this resignation and take responsibility for your awakening, no matter what?

Remember, you cannot arrive at a place that you have never left. Meaning you can never become what you are, because you have never been other than that. A famous teacher wrote a book entitled "I am That."

What is presented here is called pointing because what is presented here can be seen as true and real directly and confirmed by the authority of experience. However given the human beings are habituated to "thinking" and believing as a way of knowing, these pointings will stimulate confusion and paradox. Therefore it requires that you continue to meditate, reflect, and contemplate and have faith in the grace of the true Self that will bring you to clarity and freedom.

So if you don't get it, relax. *There is nothing to get.* Simply be present as awareness itself and see all that arises and passes from this view. There is no other possibility than to awaken to the truth of what you are because there is nothing other than that. It is only a matter of time, and if you are resolute in your quest for the truth and you are determined to realize and be what you actually are in this life, then *the possibility will be a probability.*

WHAT DOES IT ALL AMOUNT TO?

◆ ◆ ◆

In a sense, learning about Self-Realization and Non-Duality is learning about the same reality. Given that non-duality means "not two" and the Realization of the Self means the realization that there is no separate self, they both refer to the same truth. This can be confusing, and it can also be inspiring and useful. However, the only way this material can be really powerful and fulfill the possibility that it points to, is if you actually make it your business to find out who you are and what is real. This means you have to investigate Consciousness, look at what is happening in the mind and body, and then notice what is true. The pointings provided here can be of great assistance, but *only you can work out your liberation.*

When you "see" for yourself who you are and what is real, all of what is said about it seems obvious. There are no more questions. And it becomes a matter of living the truth, being the truth, and having who you are in the world be proof of the truth.

When you investigate Consciousness, practice paying attention and observing thoughts, feelings, and physical sensations moment to moment and notice what the evidence reveals. Does the evidence reveal who you are? What does watching the internal activity and how it relates to what you say, and what you do, reveal? Where are your words and deeds coming from? Are you being who you want to be in your life? In your relationships, especially with those with whom you are closest? Are you being who you want to be? Are your relationships working? Is your life working? If not, what is happening that is interfering? These are some of the questions that are part of the inquiry into who you are and what is real.

As you practice this inquiry, if you have access to a teacher of Self-inquiry and Non-Duality, he or she can assist you in avoiding mental traps and emotional disturbances that are common to this process.

If you are sincere and intent on Awakening and realizing the truth of who you are, teachers will show up in your life. You should take note when this happens and not miss the opportunity, especially if you have direct contact and access to a living teacher.

Some teachers may not be alive, yet still provide powerful support and assistance. Many of the greatest teachers continue to be available after their departure from the physical plane, in subtle forms and in writings and videos.

In the contemporary world it is common for people to have many teachers and in the end come to see that it is Awareness Itself that is the final teacher.

Imagine that you have been put under a hypnotic trance in which you were told that you would be a person that was constantly concerned and afraid of life. You were told that you were a physical body that would die and that that could happen at any moment. You were told that to be happy or satisfied you would have to have the right amount of money, the right relationship, the right possessions, and the right circumstances. You were told that you would not remember that you had been put in a trance. The only way you could come out of the trance would be to notice the trance itself, and realize that it was possible for you to be free of it. To consciously remember that you were not what you were told you were, and to recognize that fact long enough, will allow for the trance to be broken.

This need not be imagined. It is the case for human beings. We are all in a trance, sleepwalking through our lives and living inside a case of mistaken identity. It is all a pretense.

Many people notice the possibility that they could be free, but most do not follow through with the moment to moment remembering that is required to sustain it, because they get pulled back into the state of mind and the habit patterns of the illusory person, along with the tendency to ignore or forget what they noticed. Or they have a strong reactive mental state, and are afraid that they are going to lose control or believe something that is not real or true, and thus dismiss what was noticed. This is another reason to have the support of a teacher and a community of people who are aware of the truth and are committed to being Awake.

If you have seen the possibility of freedom, what will determine if you make your freedom important enough to be aware of it each and every moment? If you really see the truth, you will see that there is nothing more important than to Awaken to who you are and to live as Awareness. Anything less than that is not being alive, it is living as a state of mind, a fictitious character destined to suffer and die. This is the reality of the challenge to awaken. What is at stake is being willing to die as a person and to be what is timeless, was not born, and can never die. Can you afford the arrogance of dismissing a possibility that could offer you a Divine existence? Most people do miss it.

It is crucial to be clear that you are already Awareness, free and timeless, so to expect something to happen, or some particular experience to occur that will reveal this truth, is naive. What must be seen is that you are already Awareness, and you have merely been thinking yourself to be something other than that. It has been said that "unenlightenment is only a thought." Seeing this will open the way to the truth: You are Awareness that has taken on a limited version of your Self in order to appear in the world of diversity, the world of time and space, the world of humanity. If you recognize this, freedom is available.

Who you have taken yourself to be cannot Awaken or recognize the True Self that is Awareness Itself. Who you are as Awareness can recognize what you're not and be free.

It begins with who you have taken yourself to be trying to become who you actually are. Then, if the trying continues with an open mind, it will become apparent that your efforts are in vain, that it is not possible to become what you already are, and it will be revealed that therefore nothing needs to be done. It is at this point that the Self realizes Itself and the "peace that passeth understanding" is experienced as the home of existence.

THE THREE POSITIONS

◆ ◆ ◆

A useful way of noticing where you are in the process of Awakening and inquiry is to use the tools of observation and recognition.

There are three "ways of seeing," or positions, that one can occupy on this journey toward Self-Realization. The first position is the most common: ignorance. Meaning, you take yourself to be a person in a physical body, living in the world as a separate self, existing in time, and subject to all of the circumstances that result from this flawed premise, including your death. In this position, the person is trying to succeed in making life work and will keep repeating patterns of behavior intended to achieve stability and fulfillment.

The second position is the beginning of Self-Realization. In this position you have already had a glimpse of freedom. The recognition of the power to observe without attachment has become clear. You may be totally engrossed in some activity such that you are not aware of yourself. This is commonly called the "zone." This is different from being engrossed in a movie or TV show. Because in the case of this type of involvement you are identifying with the story or characters in the movie or TV show.

In the case of being in the zone you are not identified with what is happening, you are simply aware. In such a state there is no self-consciousness; all that appears is what is happening. For example, it is common for long distance runner to become lost in the experience of running and report an exhilarating experience that attracts them to run more often. This is a paradox because what actually happens is "You as a person are not here, so you as Awareness *are* here."

WHEN "you" ARE NOT HERE, "YOU" ARE HERE.

The ironic part of this is that nearly all of us probably experience moments of Self-Realization everyday, but we neither call it that, nor is there a self-conscious "person" present during those moments to even notice them, except in retrospect. Imagine being so engrossed with every moment of life, and there is *never* any self-conscious "person" to notice and comment on it?

Only what is happening; only Awareness.

The second position is that the possibility of Self-Realization is recognized and there is a motivation to achieve it. This is when the "seeker" comes into play.

The third position is when the recognition of the Self as the truth of who you are is confirmed sufficiently for there to be regular shifts into this experience of Being that provide a sense of peace, clarity, and fulfillment. You know as a direct experience that you are Awareness Itself. *The knowing of it is the being of it.* There will still be a seeming fluctuation between identifying as states of mind and being Awareness Itself. To practice remaining as the witness or observer will facilitate the end of what only appeared to be a process, or progression toward some endpoint. But it is seen that there was actually no process because the Self was always Itself. Awareness was always present as your True Identity. Even if there are instances when the mind comes in and emotions arise that bring forth the person as the identity, it matters not because it is realized that these are passing states occurring within the backdrop of unmoving, present Awareness. If the third position is maintained sufficiently, Awareness as the Source of *all* positions is realized and there is no longer any attention required for Realization. Life simply is living itself as the Self.

Some will find that they move from one position to another depending on what stimulates the mind and brain. This is common and will resolve itself through the active witnessing of these movements.

A NEW PSYCHOLOGY?

◆ ◆ ◆

A s I have continued working with people in the role of a psychologist, I have found that the process has dramatically changed as a result of my adapting the "direct approach" to ending psychological and emotional suffering.

It is clear to me that the most useful way to work with people is to introduce them to a direct perception of the True Self. This is a challenge, for it involves a recognition of where they are in terms of their investment in the story of the "person," and how threatened they are by the prospect of having this point of view disturbed or challenged. In some cases it is not advisable to bring this up, and it is more realistic and useful to apply conventional modes of psychotherapy. If the client matures and has the sufficient "ego strength" to let go, then it may work to introduce the possibility of Self-Realization. This is a paradox in that the identity or ego has to be strong enough or certain enough that it can be let go without fearing a loss of control. However, no one is a lost cause. It is possible for anyone to Awaken to the truth of who they are because it is already so, and in fact cannot be any other way.

There have been psychological approaches that have included

spiritual possibilities, such as the Humanistic Movement that borrowed ideas from Eastern wisdom traditions. Or Transpersonal Psychology that involves expanding the sense of self and introduces the potential of "Self-Actualization." There are also approaches that utilize meditation and Zen principles.

This approach, which is founded in Advaita teachings, is more specifically focused on the recognition of the person, or personal identity, as a false self. In other words, it points out that the "person is the problem." All psychological and emotional suffering is a result of identification as a person. All problems are "personal." When the person is seen to be an illusion, the pressure of life "happening to *me*" gives way to the freedom to be life itself. This is a non-dual approach. When the person is seen to not be real or exist in itself, the subject-object experience (a person "over here" living in a world "out there") comes to an end. Without the individual person separate and apart from everything else, all that remains is Self.

If Awakening is undertaken with support and assistance, it can eliminate the need for psychotherapy in the conventional form, as well as dependency on medications to control mental and emotional states.

I predict that this approach will continue to develop as a way of eliminating suffering and reactive behaviors, although it might not be considered a form of Psychology. It may be more accurate to consider it a form of personal evolution because it leads to freedom from the psychological structure of a person.

This form of evolution has continued to gain attention in the field. It may at some point be realized as the answer to the problem of human suffering and the destructive behaviors that continue to threaten our survival as a species.

IS THE RECOGNITION OF THE TRUE SELF ENOUGH

◆ ◆ ◆

There have been many who have questioned whether the recognition of the actual Self is enough to complete the transformation. When it is known that the Self is who you are, when this is seen clearly, is that enough to consider yourself Enlightened? Does that mean that you are the Self and there is no need for any further work or effort? Does it mean that you will now be the expression of the Self and that you are no longer capable of ignorance, ego-driven behaviors, and reactive states of mind?

These are important questions and the answer is not a simple matter because there are several factors to consider. First of all, the formation of an identity as a person, with a personality, is inevitable, so unless there is an Awakening to the True Self, the possibility of freedom, fulfillment, and a joyful life will not come into existence. The recognition of the truth is essential to open the possibility for a new life, a life of the spirit that is an unlimited expression of love. However, this recognition—while essential for the possibility to come into existence—must be stabilized, and gradually replace the patterns that continue to exist in the brain and mind. I like how Rupert Spira describes this. He says that the Self eventually colonizes the identity. If this process does not occur, the Realization will be incomplete and the Self will be merely another "experience" that happened in time and will become a memory that will have little or no impact on one's actual life.

In other words, if the Awakening and Recognition begins a process of transformation wherein the limited personal identity drops away over time, then the person shows up as an expression of Awareness Itself. If, however, the Awakening does not result in a consistent knowing of Self as Awareness, there may still be knowledge of the Self, and a conclusion that the person *is* the Self, but that alone does not change the tendencies to behave in ego-driven ways. This can be dangerous because such a person can imagine that they are Enlightened and superior to other human beings, which can become a twisted delusion that permits all kinds of immoral behaviors, justified as "lessons" to challenge or Awaken seekers. Or it can be a way of bypassing aspects of psychological pathology by creating a superior spiritual identity.

The recognition that the True Self is Awareness, and the relief, freedom, and peace that is inherent to this recognition, is not the complete Realization. The Realization is complete when there is a continuous knowing of Self-as-Awareness, so that even if patterns arise from the brain and mind that have not yet dissolved, they are seen for what they are and not given credibility. Then the Realization is sufficient to be reliable enough to not result in ignorant, ego-driven behaviors.

It is important to be clear that Self-Realization is a *way of being in the world*, not just an interior recognition. Incomplete Realization can be a source of much confusion and be extremely misleading to those who follow teachers that have mistaken an elevated and "spiritualized" ego-identity for their True Self.

PRACTICAL
STRATEGIES

◆ ◆ ◆

There are some ways to increase the probability of being aware of the Self and to gradually reside as the Self. It is essential to practice paying attention to (being mindful of) the tendency to identify with thoughts, feelings, and physical sensations so that certain strategies can be utilized.

One strategy is to recognize "complaining," whether it is complaining to others or complaining by just perpetually thinking about what is wrong or what should be different; i.e., resisting the way it is. Complaining is one of the ways the personality manifests. It expresses a point of view that is self-righteous, and this reinforces the idea of who one considers oneself to be. To notice the tendency to complain and to seek agreement from others about complaints is to be aware of the personality in action.

In fact, the tendency to "seek agreement" is yet another problematic aspect of personal psychology. This is a way to confirm the identity by confirming its point of view. When people agree on their point of view it provides a sense of certainty about reality, and part of that reality is the existence of the separate person.

When there is collective agreement by most of human society about the presumed limited nature of personal identity, it creates a very solid belief system about who we are that is very difficult to pierce. This business of seeking agreement is particularly important to maintain a sense of security by identifying with a viewpoint, belief, or philosophy that provides not only a sense of belonging, but also a sense of being "real," as a person connected to other people.

Spending time alone and in silence is useful. This strategy eliminates the tendency to use the familiar ways of being and interacting that maintain the sense of the person. In addition, it provides an opportunity to notice the play of the mind, i.e. repetitious thoughts about the past or the future along with apprehension.

Along the same lines, practicing meditation can be useful if it is understood that meditation is an opportunity to notice Awareness and directly witness the activity of the mind, particularly as it relates to the generation and maintenance of the personality. If the person is practicing meditation to achieve a higher consciousness or escape stress and suffering, while they may very well succeed, and reduce stress via learning to relax the body and calm the mind, the existence of the person will be continued and the actual source of suffering missed.

Studying the wisdom traditions can provide a solid foundation of information that can motivate the process of Self-Realization and confirm the fact that the truth of who we are has been available, unchanged, for thousands of years, taught through many different forms and practices around the world. Today, with the advent of the Internet, students of the wisdom traditions have access to more teachers and teachings than ever before.

Psychotherapy can still be a useful strategy for people who need to develop the sense of safety that comes with ego strength. As previously mentioned, the person has to be mature enough and have enough of a secure sense of self (personality) to let go. This letting go is dropping the dependence on the familiar ways of being, and trusting that no harm will come of it.

Being part of a community committed to Self-Realization can be a very empowering strategy. If it is a community founded on being a container that supports Awakening and does not require allegiance to a specific leader and provides support, compassion, and acceptance, it can accelerate Awakening.

ABOUT THE AUTHOR

E arly on in my life I had a strong sense that I was more than my circumstances. This led me through many turns on the road of life, some of which were useful and some of which were very painful and difficult. On several occasions during my childhood and my adult years I stumbled into distinctly different states of consciousness that were complete and fulfilling in every way. I was certain that these states must be more intentionally accessible. The experiences I had were ones in which I was totally myself, with full knowledge of life, and a calm, loving, and joyful interest in all that appeared before me. For most of my life, I have considered those experiences to be moments of what is called Enlightenment. And yet they came and went. Then at some point a timeless experience took me over, and I came to see that the previous experiences were merely temporary states of mind that were unencumbered by the typical noise, confusion, and distractions of life, yet incomplete in some sense. This timeless experience was *unchanging,* and was a Ground of Being that was untouched by ever-changing states of mind.

I worked in prisons for thirty-two years as a teacher, psychologist, and administrator. This environment was a dramatic learning experience. I witnessed human cruelty, sadistic guards, inmates that preyed upon each other, and an indifferent, ignorant, and a profoundly corrupt system. The world inside the prisons was so brutal and bizarre that it shook me deeply and I felt a commitment to somehow help prisoners realize the possibility of being psychologically and emotionally free, so that they could live a lawful life and escape the revolving doors of the prison system.

I implemented and personally led programs for prisoners, providing them access to teachings and practices from the Human Potential Movement and various Eastern wisdom schools that offered a transformational experience. Over the years I studied and practiced various forms of meditation, and read and studied the works of many Eastern and Western teachers. Among the works that influenced me the most were the writings of Carlos Castaneda, Alan Watts, J. Krishnamurti, and George Gurdjieff. I have been a student of Werner Erhard since 1973 and have delivered much of his material in programs for inmates. I've also continued to study and benefit from the access the Internet provides to current teachers of both mindfulness and especially the direct path to Self-Realization.

Following my career in the prison system, I worked in a psychiatric residential program providing treatment for people with severe mental disorders. Here I learned more about how the mind can become so dysfunctional that the person is at odds with the collective reality.

More recently, I have a small private psychotherapy practice, and I also teach meditation, T'ai Chi Chih (a form of Qigong, an energy movement practice). I continue to write and provide gatherings to share an approach to addressing psychological issues with non-dual teachings.

The heart of my work combines fifty years of conventional psychology with leading-edge work in human potential and transformation, and contemporary forms of teaching and practicing Self-Realization.

It is clear to me that the true gift in life is the experience of making a difference in the lives of others and contributing to the well-being of humanity.

OTHER BOOKS: ENLIGHTENMENT MADE EASY,
Amazon ebook and paperback.

YOUTUBE: Channel: DRDPARRISH48

WEBSITE: DRDAVIDPARRISH.COM

EMAIL: DR.D.PARRISH@GMAIL.COM

Notes